ALSO BY TIM PEAKE

Hello, is this planet Earth? (2016)
Ask an Astronaut (2018)
The Astronaut Selection Test Book (2019)
Limitless: The Autobiography (2021)
Swarm Rising (2021) (with Steve Cole)
Swarm Enemy (2022) (with Steve Cole)

First published in Great Britain in 2022 by Wren & Rook
This paperback edition published in Great Britain in 2023

Text copyright ©Tim Peake, 2022
Illustration copyright © Max Rambaldi, 2022

PB ISBN: 978 1 5263 6491 3
E-book ISBN: 978 1 5263 6362 6
1 3 5 7 9 10 8 6 4 2

MIX
Paper from
responsible sources
FSC® C104740

Wren & Rook
An imprint of
Hachette Children's Group

Part of Hodder & Stoughton
Carmelite House
50 Victoria Embankment
London EC4Y 0DZ

An Hachette UK Company
www.hachette.co.uk
www.hachettechildrens.co.uk

Printed in China

Designed by Nigel Baines
Additional images supplied by Nigel Baines
With thanks to Christine Tursky

The website addresses (URLs) included in this book were valid at the time
of going to press. However, it is possible that contents or addresses
may have changed since the publication of this book.

THE COSMIC DIARY OF OUR INCREDIBLE UNIVERSE

TIM PEAKE

With STEVE COLE

Illustrated by Max Rambaldi

wren
&rook

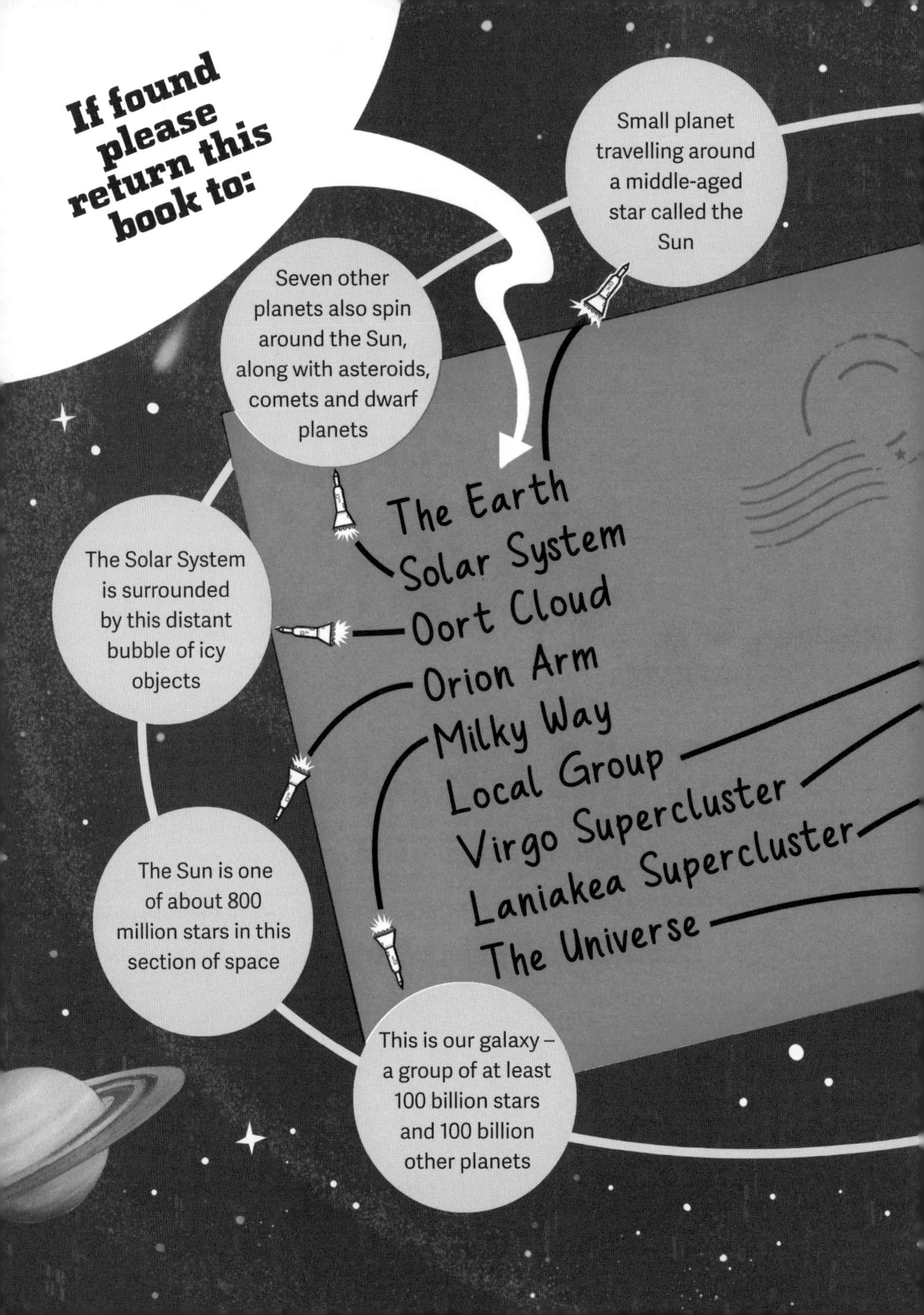
If found please return this book to:
Small planet travelling around a middle-aged star called the Sun
Seven other planets also spin around the Sun, along with asteroids, comets and dwarf planets
The Solar System is surrounded by this distant bubble of icy objects
The Sun is one of about 800 million stars in this section of space
This is our galaxy – a group of at least 100 billion stars and 100 billion other planets
The Earth
Solar System
Oort Cloud
Orion Arm
Milky Way
Local Group
Virgo Supercluster
Laniakea Supercluster
The Universe

About 80 small galaxies spin slowly around the Milky Way and the galaxy next door, Andromeda

This contains about 100 small groups of galaxies including the Local Group

Pronounced 'lah-nee-ah-keh-ah' this huge structure contains 100,000 galaxies

Beyond these superclusters, the Universe contains at least 2 trillion other galaxies!

Contents

Introduction

Imagine floating in space, with no forces acting on your body. Your muscles are completely relaxed and there is no sound, except for a small hum from a pump sending oxygen into your spacesuit, keeping you alive. It's the most peaceful feeling imaginable.

Over one shoulder you see a **beautiful planet**, full of colour: blue oceans, white clouds, orange deserts and green forests. That's Earth. That's where you were born. The planet itself looks alive – electrical storms light up the night sky, volcanoes leave trails of smoke, **swirling hurricanes** form over **warm oceans** and the eerie lights of the aurora dance over the poles. It's comforting to look at. It's home.

You look over the other shoulder. It's black. In fact, it's the blackest black you have ever seen. It's so dark you feel like you are falling into it, being sucked towards an **infinite black universe**. It's not comforting to look at. In fact, it's quite scary.

As you **effortlessly** orbit the Earth you pass from daylight to night. The Sun quickly sets and suddenly the Universe comes alive. Stars appear over the horizon and you can see the familiar planets of Venus, Mars, Jupiter and Saturn. Hundreds of billions of stars now come into view, shining their pinpricks of light through the blackness.

Your mind is trying to make sense of what you are seeing. On the one hand, looking out into endless space, you feel so **incredibly small**, so insignificant.

After all, **your planet** is just a small lump of rock orbiting a very ordinary star.

We call that star 'the Sun' like it's something special. But in fact the Sun is simply one of at least **100 billion** stars that make up the Milky Way – a very average-sized galaxy, and one of an estimated **2 trillion galaxies** that exist.

The Earth and all its neighbours orbiting the Sun – our entire solar system – could be **snuffed out** and, frankly, the Universe would barely even notice the difference.

Or would it?

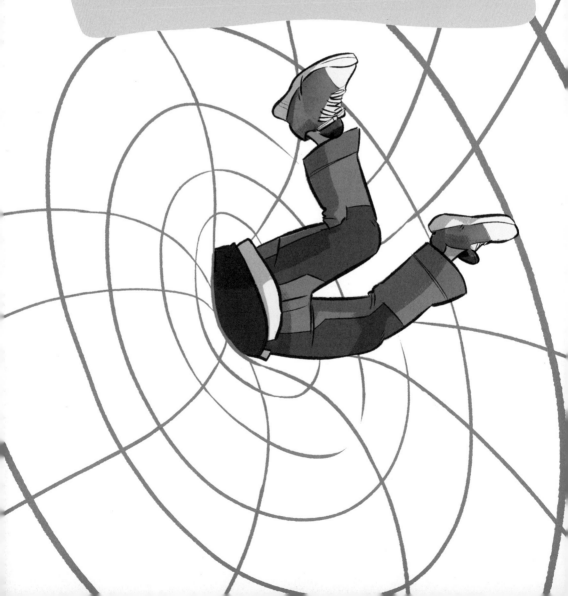

To answer that, the first thing we need to do is travel back in time. So jump in, hold on tight, wind the clock back **13.8 billion years**. All the way to the beginning, and **then** pop back just a little bit further. Things are going to get pretty weird, because where we are going it seems that absolutely **NOTHING** exists.

No light.

No sound.

No time.

No space.

No school.

Just, yes – you got it . . .

NOTHING.

So . . . just what happened to turn that nothing into **SOMETHING**?

Well, just as you might keep a diary of all the things you've done in your life, so the Universe has left a record of how it began and how it's changed over time. Every time you look up at the stars you **look into the past**, because those stars are so far away that their light takes thousands, millions or even **billions** of years to reach us. With telescopes we can see further out into space – further back through time. If we know what we're looking for we can see all the way back to the Universe's beginning . . . and work out how it might finish up.

This book is a cosmic diary of our incredible Universe, but in a way it is **YOUR** diary. So, it doesn't matter if you peek inside and read a bit . . . right?

It's time for the Universe to reveal its secrets.

So let's take a peek!

Look out for the symbol
Whenever you see it, you'll learn more about a cosmic curiosity!

Meet the Experts

Particle Physicist: Malika

Hi, I'm Malika, and I'm a particle physicist! You may not have heard of 'particles' before, but they are tiny pieces of something. I study the tiniest building blocks of matter (the stuff that everything in the Universe is made of), and I help to develop and test theories about how the particles behave and interact. Particle physicists are really important to understanding how our Universe came to be!

Cosmologists: Ben and Ciara

Hello, I'm Ciara. And I'm Ben. We are both cosmologists! Our job is to explore and investigate the nature of the Universe. We study the creation and evolution of our cosmos and try to predict and understand what the future of the Universe will be. Cosmologists use and interpret data a lot. We look forward to explaining facts about the cosmos to you!

Astronaut Tim

Hi there, Tim here! I'm an astronaut for the European Space Agency (ESA), and I was the first British astronaut to visit the International Space Station (ISS). During my six-month mission on the ISS, I conducted a spacewalk, ran the London marathon from the space station's treadmill, took part in over 250 scientific experiments and engaged with more than 1.6 million schoolchildren in over 30 scientific projects. It's great to see you here, and I look forward to explaining more about space as you read on!

17

BANG!

I'M HERE!

Dear Diary,

Today began a bit weirdly when, all of a sudden, I just POPPED into existence! Call it what you want — magic, or a miracle, or some mysterious law of nature — but one minute there was nothing and then there was something . . .

And boy, did I create **HAVOC** on my arrival.

I burst in on the scene as just a mega-ultra-super-teeny-weeny speck and then grew at least a gazillion times larger in just a tiny fraction of a second.

Put another way, that speck of the Universe was infinitesimally small – and expanded in an infinitesimally short space of time! And guess what? That infinitesimally short space of time was actually the beginning of space and time. Now I can stretch out and grow older.

All in all, that's a pretty impressive start to my existence. And I think I'm going to be around for a loooooooooooooooooooooooooooooooooooooooooooooooooooooooooooooooooooooooooooooooooooooooooong time . . .

WHERE DOES YOUR STORY BEGIN?

You were born here on the Earth. You're one of the planet's roughly **8 billion human beings**. But how did you end up on this planet? How did this planet get here and why is it orbiting a star, in a spiral arm of a galaxy called the Milky Way, in a far-flung corner of what we call the Universe?

The reason for it all lies back at the very **beginning of time**.

Try really hard to imagine **NOTHING**. Now imagine that all of a sudden something happened.

Something INCREDIBLE happened.

Imagine floating around surrounded by absolute NOTHINGNESS and then all of sudden – **BAM** – a universe appears out of nowhere!

This moment of creation has become known as the **BIG BANG**. It actually wasn't that big and there was no bang, because there was nothing for any sound to travel through. But to be fair, it was still a pretty impressive beginning.

Within **0.00000000000000000000000000 00000001 seconds** the Universe went from being a tiny, hot, dense speck many billions of times smaller than the full stop at the end of this sentence to something the size of a grapefruit.

That might not sound like much, but it's basically the same as a marble expanding to **10 million times** the width of the Milky Way in a tiny fraction of a second.

This is known as **cosmic inflation**.

Utterly mind-boggling, isn't it? Cosmologists like me are here to explore and explain the nature of the Universe, and — I must tell you — we struggled to make sense of **cosmic inflation** for many years. The rate of expansion was so great and happened so quickly that it appeared to exceed the speed of light — a universal speed limit that cannot be broken.

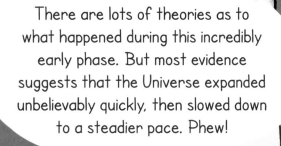

However, some bright spark realised that this speed-of-light limit does not apply to the expansion of space itself . . . So, the Universe was NOT arrested for speeding!

There are lots of theories as to what happened during this incredibly early phase. But most evidence suggests that the Universe expanded unbelievably quickly, then slowed down to a steadier pace. Phew!

How can we tell the age of the Universe?

It takes some very careful measuring . . . and a lot of number crunching! One technique is to estimate the age of the oldest stars. A more accurate way is to measure the present rate of the Universe's expansion and work backwards. Using vast amounts of data gathered from powerful probes and telescopes, different space agencies have arrived at slightly different dates. But they all suggest that the Universe is in the region of 13.8 billion years old.

WHAT CAUSED THE BIG BANG?

Experts think that at the **Beginning Of All Things** the fundamental forces of nature were bundled together as a single, unified force. It may have been the breakdown of this unified force that gave the Universe the 'kick' needed for the Big Bang to occur.

There are four fundamental forces that govern everything that happens in the Universe. I know your mind is already getting blown, but don't worry, I'll explain these as we go through!

1. ELECTROMAGNETISM
2. WEAK NUCLEAR FORCE
3. STRONG NUCLEAR FORCE
4. GRAVITY

SMALL BUT NOT (YET) PERFECTLY FORMED . . .

Whatever kicked things off, the **crazy speed** of cosmic inflation was vital for **YOUR** existence. If the Universe had expanded more slowly, its temperature would have been perfectly uniform and all its ingredients neatly and evenly laid out. As it turned out, tiny variations in the make-up of the miniscule Universe would prove vital later on. These variations led to regions that were richer in the exotic particles that would eventually allow stars and galaxies and planets to form.

So without these early flaws in the just-born Universe, **none of us would be here**. And space as we observe it today would not exist either. It just goes to show, nobody's perfect – and thank goodness for that!

All the matter and energy that will ever exist in the entire Universe was squashed into this tiny beginning. How come? Because the weird conditions that created the Big Bang made it possible!

What is space?

Space is basically what it sounds like – space! Space is the airless vacuum in which every galaxy, star and planet exists. On Earth we say that outer space begins about 100 kilometres above sea level at the Kármán line – this is the point where our planet's atmosphere runs out. It's easy to think of space being full of nothing. But it's actually full of particles, energy, light, heat, gas, rocks, ice and loads of other stuff. Including a lot of stuff that we know must be there but just cannot see, like dark matter and dark energy.

WHAT WAS THERE BEFORE THE BIG BANG?

The simple answer is – we don't know for sure. This is a difficult thing for us humans to get our heads around, because our minds understand everything in terms of beginnings and endings. But even asking the question of what came before the Big Bang doesn't make sense, because there was no time before the Big Bang.

It's a bit like asking what lies south of the South Pole? **NOTHING.** It's impossible to answer. That's one reason why so many different theories have sprung up around what started the Big Bang. But whether you believe the Universe was created by God, a quirk of science or a teenage alien kid in another universe who made us all up in a simulated game, the simple answer is that **no one knows for sure**.

We may never truly understand what was there before the Big Bang, or just how the Universe came into being. Perhaps one day, **YOU** can help to answer that question.

Meanwhile, in trying to learn the truth, we have uncovered and solved so many other mysteries …

JOURNEY THROUGH SPACE

In our imaginations we can travel anywhere, as we will in this book. But in real life, the only way we know to journey through space is in a spaceship …

The word 'spaceship' makes us think of sailing across an ocean of space. And the word **'astronaut'** in Greek literally means a 'star sailor'. In fact, there are many similarities between a spaceship and a sailing ship. Both vessels are designed to protect us, to keep us alive in a **hostile** environment and to carry us safely from one place to another.

What's more, both ships are being **pulled by gravity**. A sailing ship is designed to float on water, to stop the force of gravity from sinking it. A spaceship is designed with thrusters – it needs some sort of propulsion system to stop gravity from pulling it in a direction it shouldn't be going in. And whereas a sailing ship can catch the wind in its sails, some future spaceships might also be able to catch the 'wind' in their sails too. However, in space the **wind is not molecules of air**, but streams of charged particles flying away from the Sun, and the sails are big mirrors bombarded by these particles.

But there's only one place in space we know of that has exactly the right conditions to keep you alive as you whizz through it … and **you're standing on it** (or maybe sitting or lying down on it) right now! That's right, it's the incredible **Spaceship Earth**.

Even with all its problems, there's no better place to be that we know of!

Can you ever reach the edge of the Universe?

The Universe doesn't have real edges – that would imply that the Universe has a centre too, like an enormous map. But the Universe isn't built that way, because the **Big Bang** was not like a real explosion that starts from a single point. The Big Bang happened everywhere all at once. The Universe is expanding equally from every point.

It might help to imagine dots drawn on the surface of a balloon. As you blow up the balloon all the dots move further apart from all the other dots. If you think of each dot as a galaxy, you can picture how they move away from each other.

In a way, though, **YOU** are the centre of the Universe – because wherever you might be, it appears as if all of space is expanding away from YOU. It's like if you could sit inside a ball of dough with raisins in, rising in an oven. Wherever you sit, the raisins would seem to be moving away from you in all directions.

Now, get out of there, **it's far too hot.** Ugh, now you're all covered in dough and raisins! Clean yourself up and we'll move onto the **next chapter** …

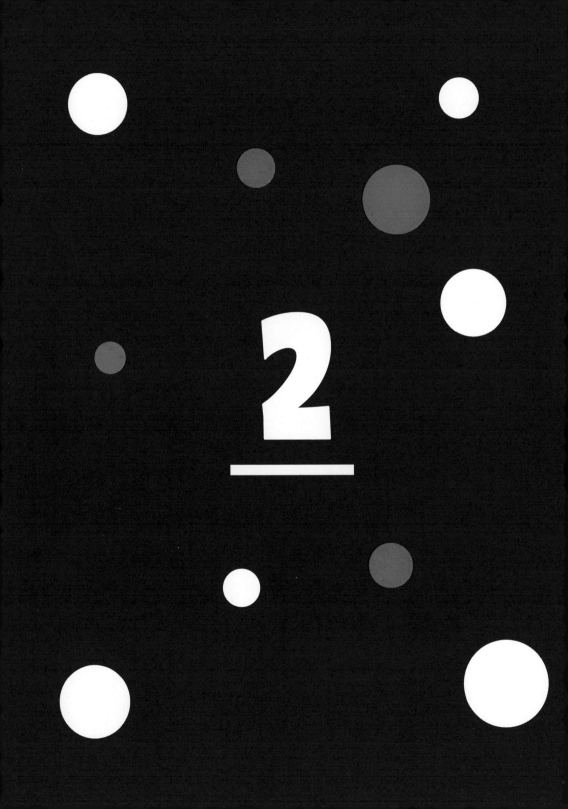

BATTLE
OF THE
PARTICLES

Dear Diary,

Less than 1 second old

I got into a massive fight today. I'm still only a fraction of a second old and I'm already causing trouble. **But it wasn't my fault**, honest . . . For a start I couldn't see anything, since I still have no light!

And then I got caught up in this crazy battle between two rival gangs: matter and antimatter. I tried to solve it peacefully, but they weren't interested in talking. Instead, they tried to annihilate each other in a monumental

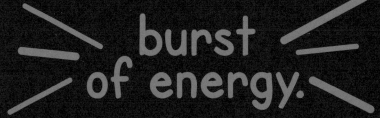

burst of energy.

After all the effort I had put into creating the Big Bang, the first thing these particles want to do is wipe each other out!

THE FIRST THINGS THAT MATTER

As the Universe expanded rapidly in the Big Bang, **it began to cool**.

This was bound to happen. **Particles are small bits of matter that make up everything in the Universe.** They heat up when moving around – bumping and jostling into each other – and the **faster they move, the more heat they create**. When the Universe was small, the particles bashed together the whole time so they were super-hot. It's a bit like a crowd of people huddled together at a football match. They share each other's warmth when they stand close together, but what happens when the crowd disperses at the end of the match? They have no one to share warmth with so they start to feel cooler.

Have you ever found a 'skin' on your custard or gravy or hot chocolate? You might say **'yuck'**, but that's what happens as the liquid cools. As the Universe cooled, the first matter formed – tiny particles with funny names like **quarks, electrons, photons and neutrinos**. Without them, **nothing we know in the Universe would exist** . . .

HOWEVER, matter had a fight on its hands. Because as matter formed, so did its arch-rival antimatter!

Just like light is the opposite of dark and day is the opposite of night, antimatter is the opposite of matter. Both contain tiny particles, but antimatter particles are the reverse of regular matter particles. As a result, when matter and antimatter particles collided, they caused **explosions that destroyed each other**.

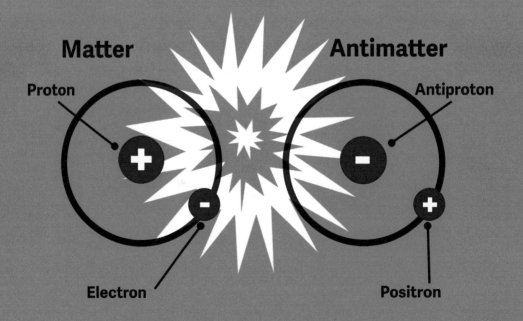

Because there was slightly more matter than antimatter – about **one particle per billion more** – it meant that matter won the big battle and survived!

Minute specks of antimatter can still form when certain chemicals decay. This happens in bananas — and also in YOU! But don't worry, it's a teeny-tiny, miniscule reaction. No danger of exploding bananas (or people!).

39

Dear Diary,

Still less than 1 second old

Matter JUST won the fight against antimatter. Which I guess is a good job, since without any matter you wouldn't be reading this now. Anyway, all that energy released in the fight didn't go to waste. It's causing me to keep expanding (like I need that after the whole 'cosmic inflation' thing!). I don't know where all this growing is leading to but at some point it surely has to stop . . .

doesn't it?

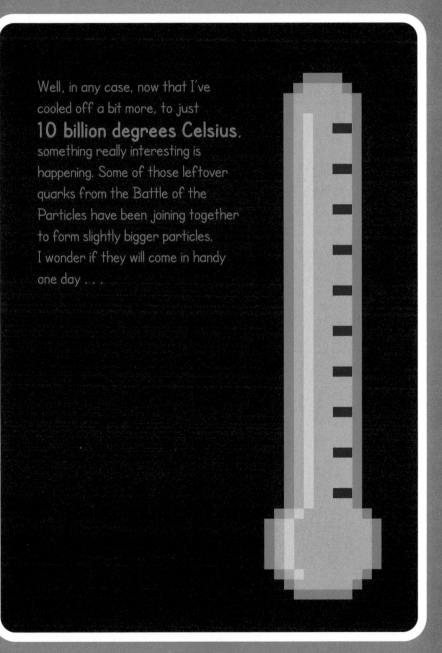

Well, in any case, now that I've cooled off a bit more, to just **10 billion degrees Celsius**, something really interesting is happening. Some of those leftover quarks from the Battle of the Particles have been joining together to form slightly bigger particles. I wonder if they will come in handy one day . . .

QUARK SOUP

So, even though the Universe started cooling, it was still about 10 billion degrees Celsius! It was still small enough that all the particles of matter inside it were close together like a thick 'soup'. Electrons went on whizzing about in that **super-hot soup of particles**, and within a few millionths of a second quarks joined together to produce new particles called protons and neutrons. The ingredients in the soup were changing! Within minutes, these protons and neutrons joined together too in different ways to make something new and exciting.

Dear Diary,

3 minutes old

I know I'm still incredibly young, but I feel like I've grown up a lot. I can still be a bit hot headed — in fact it's about a billion degrees Celsius in here — but I've calmed down enough to REALLY make something of myself. Because guess what? If I take some really tiny particles and smash them together — BOOM! — I start creating atomic nuclei, which are the building blocks of ATOMS.

And I reckon that, in about 300,000 years' time, atoms will turn out to be the building blocks of EVERYTHING. This could be the start of something BIG . . .

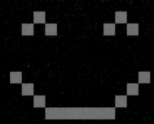

Around **three minutes** into the creation of the Universe, protons and neutrons started making the nuclei of hydrogen and helium atoms – some of the very first chemical elements! But the atoms were not stable. The Universe was filled with a hot, dense mixture of atomic nuclei and electrons all jumbled up together – a searingly hot, gassy mixture known as **plasma**.

Say 'nuclei' as 'NEW-KLEE-EYE'.

Nuclei is simply the plural of the word 'nucleus' – the central, most important part of something.

BASIC ELEMENTS OF LIFE

When baking your **favourite chocolate cake**, you use heat from the oven to transform a mix of ingredients into something new. The Universe did something similar to make atomic nuclei. It took protons and neutrons and 'baked' them together, first to make **hydrogen nuclei** and then to make **helium nuclei**, and later on other types of nuclei as well.

This 'baking' process is called **nuclear fusion** (think of fusing protons and neutrons together to make nuclei). Hydrogen and helium nuclei are the easiest ones to make so they came first.

Nuclear fusion is only possible at really high temperatures – far, far higher than you'd find in any oven! Even though it starts hot, nuclear fusion makes things even hotter because it releases more energy when particles or nuclei fuse together.

Dear Diary,

370,000 years old

Wow – it seems like ages since I last wrote, but there was a lot of cleaning up to do after those **crazy** first few seconds of my life. I'm still expanding, which is causing things to cool down even more around here. In fact, I'm just a balmy **2,700 degrees Celsius** now!

But something incredible has happened.

Remember how I made **atomic nuclei** by fusing protons and neutrons together? It turns out nuclei feel a bit unbalanced on their own, but when they team up with electrons they form **stable atoms**.

Everything feels much calmer now. AND I am the very proud owner of loads of **hydrogen** and **helium** atoms! They are going to be so useful when I start making **stars**.

Atoms fit together with other atoms to make all the different things in the Universe — from stars to hot chocolate to anteaters. Atoms are so small that about 500,000 atoms can fit within the thickness of a human hair.

INSIDE AN ATOM

As we know, atoms are the building blocks of everything in the Universe! Protons and neutrons form the nucleus of an atom and electrons spin around the nucleus. Here are the components that make up an atom:

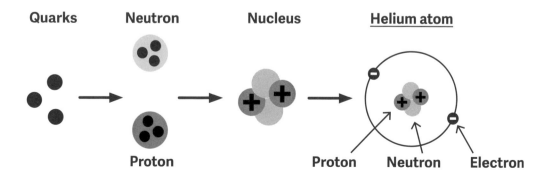

Quarks   Neutron   Nucleus   **Helium atom**

Proton   Proton   Neutron   Electron

There's a **special force** that acts like a glue to keep the parts of an atom together. This force that holds neutrons and protons together in an atomic nucleus is called the **strong nuclear force**. It's also the force that allows quarks to stick together to form protons and neutrons. The strong nuclear force is one of the four universal forces we began to explore earlier (see page 26). Now that we can make atoms, we are well on the way to making **every single thing** you can think of in the Universe!

Have you heard the saying 'opposites attract'? It's true about protons and electrons! (It's true about poles of a magnet too — because electromagnetism, another one of the four universal forces, is responsible!)

STABLE ATOMS

No, not that sort of stable, silly!

There's something interesting about protons and electrons: they both have a tiny electrical charge. The **proton** has a positive charge and the **electron** has a negative charge. Neutrons have no charge – but don't worry, they don't feel left out! They just help to balance out the protons and electrons so that the atoms feel stable.

After the Universe cooled to about **3,000 degrees Celsius**, atoms were able to collect the electrons they needed to balance out the positive charge caused by the protons in the nuclei.

Balancing these charges let the atoms become stable. At this point the first chemical elements in the Universe were formed: **hydrogen** (which made up about 75 per cent of matter in the Universe) and **helium** (which made up about 24 per cent of matter in the Universe).

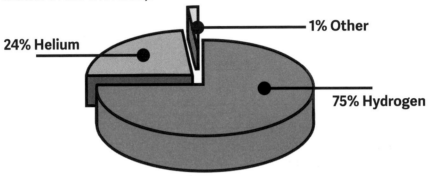

24% Helium

1% Other

75% Hydrogen

A hydrogen atom is the simplest of all and that's why so much of it was created. It has one proton in the nucleus with one electron spinning around it.

A helium atom has two protons and two neutrons in the nucleus, with two electrons spinning around it.

Traces of other elements soon followed (which is the remaining 1 per cent of matter in the Universe). The varying number of protons and neutrons inside elements is what makes each one unique.

Are atoms the same everywhere?

Even though atoms combine with other atoms to make different things, each type of atom is always the same. A hydrogen atom inside a human being is the same as a hydrogen atom inside the Sun – they are just combined with other atoms in different ways.

Did you notice that an atom has the same number of protons and electrons? That's so the positive and negative charges are equal and balance each other out!

The coming of atoms meant that the **young Universe** would never be the same again. Things were going to change in a **BIG** way.

LET THERE BE
LIGHT
(AND DARK)

Dear Diary,

380,000 years old

Remember my big fight between matter and antimatter? Well, it released **LOADS** of energy – including **HUGE** numbers of photons. Photons are particles of light energy.

For years those photons have been trapped in plasma. But now that I'm full of atoms, things have calmed down and those photons can travel around freely. This is a BIG deal, Diary – it's called

 LIGHT

. . . Surely someone can see me now?

BEGINNING TO SEE THE LIGHT

As the Universe expanded and cooled down some more, the crazy chaos of that hot, dense soup of particles became more ordered. Quarks and electrons were hoovered up to make stable atoms, and **photons** finally had some room to move around. As a result, the Universe was no longer bathed in darkness and became transparent. In other words, if any of us had been there we'd be able to see through it! More photons were created, and instead of being stuck in plasma they could travel through space.

Photons are tiny bundles of electromagnetic energy. This is a type of energy that is made of electrical and magnetic waves that can travel through space. Yep, it's electromagnetism again! Where would we be without it? In the dark, for a start!

Photons brought the first light in the Universe. Scientists say that if you could have seen it, some of this 'first light' would have been visible as a **bright** and **warm**, **white glow**. However, it would have felt like being trapped in an oven at about **2,700 degrees Celsius**, so you wouldn't have hung around for long!

'FLAVOURS' OF LIGHT

Light isn't just something that keeps away the dark. Photons each contain a particular amount of energy, so light is itself a type of **energy** and it travels through the Universe as **electromagnetic waves**.

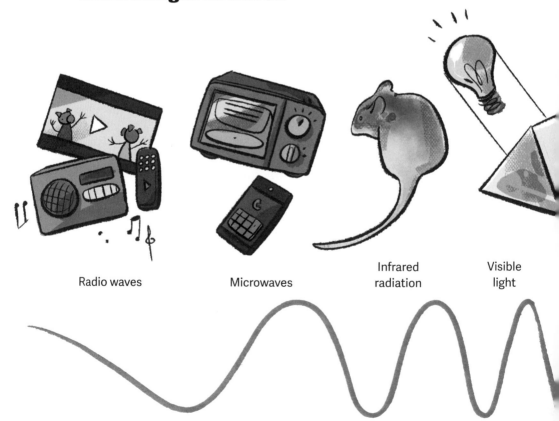

| Radio waves | Microwaves | Infrared radiation | Visible light |

You might be wondering, why is light made up of many different colours? And why can't we see infrared light or ultraviolet light?

Have a look at the illustration below. The waves are basically wiggles. As you can see, some light has very long wavelengths and some has really short wavelengths. The length of the wiggles (wavelengths) depends on the amount of energy in the photons that make the electromagnetic wave.

ELECTROMAGNETIC SPECTRUM

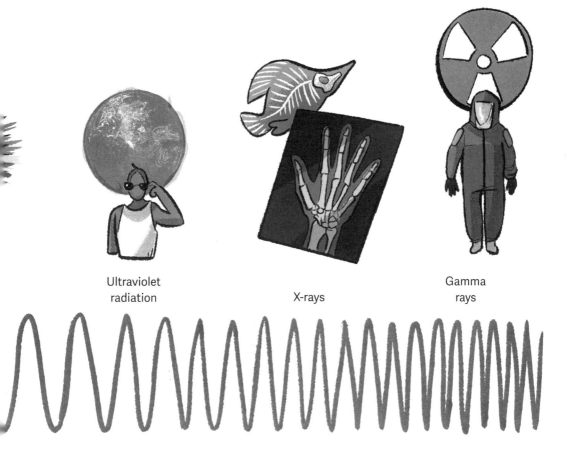

Ultraviolet radiation

X-rays

Gamma rays

Visible light – the spectrum of colours that we can see (such as when we see a rainbow) – has wavelengths that are around the middle of the spectrum, and different wavelengths within that range give us the different colours.

Other forms of 'light', such as **X-rays** or **radio waves**, have shorter or longer wavelengths than visible light. Shorter wavelengths like X-rays are comprised of photons with higher energy than visible light. Longer wavelengths like radio waves are comprised of photons with lower energy than visible light. While we can't see the whole electromagnetic spectrum with our eyes, science has taught us how we can still use different wavelengths of 'light' for all sorts of useful things.

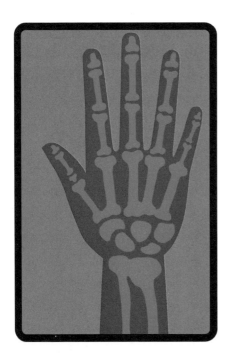

If you break a bone, the hospital will give you an X-ray – a form of light we use to see through things. X-rays are used to see inside your bags at the airport, too. If you listen to a radio, you are *hearing* 'light' in the form of radio waves translated into sound. **Microwaves** heat up your dinner – they are another wavelength of light energy that is powerful but which we can't actually see.

All these photons travelling freely through the Universe also give us different ways to see and try to understand how the Universe was created and how it behaves. We can use vast and powerful telescopes that harness different parts of the electromagnetic spectrum to peer deep into the Universe. There are many **famous telescopes** on Earth and in space. Here are a few:

• **The Hubble Space Telescope** is in orbit around the Earth and can detect visible light. It lets us see stars and other objects much further away than we can see from Earth because the Hubble doesn't have to look through the Earth's atmosphere.

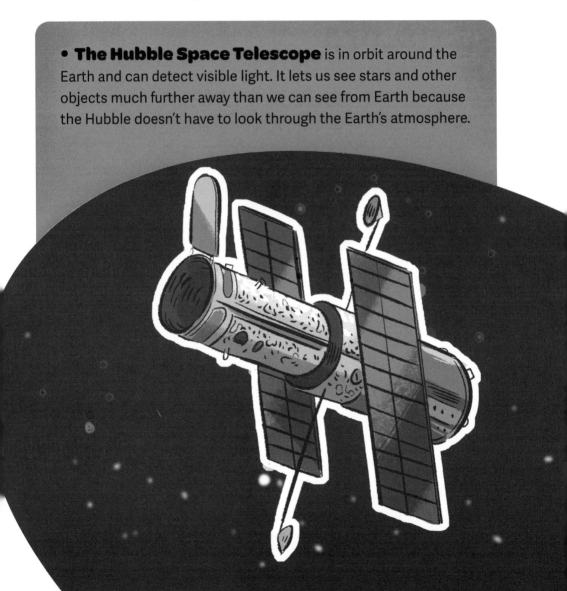

- **The Chandra Space Telescope** developed by NASA uses X-rays and is currently orbiting Earth as a satellite.

- **The Spitzer Space Telescope** was the third spacecraft dedicated to infrared astronomy, using infrared light on its missions.

- **The Arecibo Telescope** in Puerto Rico, a US island in the Caribbean Sea, used radio waves and was in operation for 57 years.

By letting us examine different wavelengths of electromagnetic energy, all these different telescopes help us learn about the Universe and can look at objects far outside our own galaxy.

We can't see infrared light, but did you know that we can feel it on our skin? We feel infrared light as warmth.

THE COSMIC MICROWAVE BACKGROUND

The Universe has been expanding since the Big Bang. And that means that the 'first light' of the Universe has also changed.

It's easy to see why.

Draw a wiggly wavelength on a thick rubber band, and then stretch the rubber band. Do you see how the wave gets stretched as well?

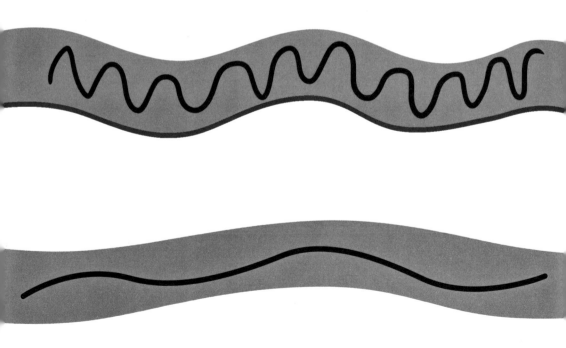

This is what happened to the 'first light' – which was emitted as photons of visible light and heat. As this light travelled through an expanding Universe, it was stretched out like the wave drawn on a rubber band. The visible light waves were stretched into infrared waves as the Universe kept expanding, and then stretched even more into microwaves. We can't see microwaves with the naked eye but we can detect them using special equipment.

Today we call that light the **Cosmic Microwave Background** – or the CMB. Because the CMB was the first light in the Universe, it gave us strong evidence that the Universe began with the Big Bang, and without the Big Bang, none of us would be here!

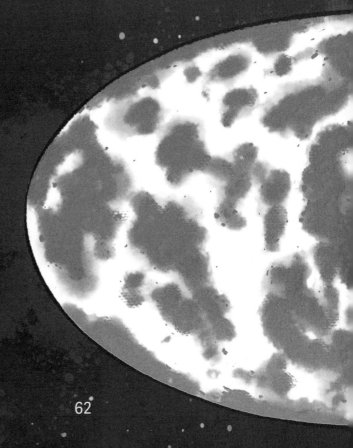

What do pigeons have to do with the Cosmic Microwave Background?

The Cosmic Microwave Background was discovered in 1964 by astronomers in New Jersey, USA. They picked up a strange 'hiss', which they thought was an annoying malfunction caused by pigeon poo on their antenna. What they had actually detected was that 'first light' of the Universe, from 13.8 billion years ago.

This image shows the whole sky. The patches show the CMB. Why is it patchy? Well, remember at the very beginning of the Universe there were tiny fluctuations – which meant that things were not evenly spread out.

Dear Diary,

400,000 years old

Well, what do you know? Just as it was all getting started, someone turned out the lights. I keep expanding, which is causing me to cool down; that lovely warm plasma has been extinguished.

Is this the end? I can't help feeling cold, dark and lifeless . . .

THE COSMIC DARK AGES

So, as the Universe expanded, the 'first light' was stretched until it would no longer have been visible. It also continued to cool. You may remember that as matter cooled it created elements – mostly hydrogen and helium. But that was just a tiny amount of the matter in the Universe. Most of the matter that existed during this phase was **dark matter**.

What is dark matter? 'Dark' is a very good name for it, because it doesn't interact with electromagnetic waves – that means it's made of particles that do not reflect, emit or absorb light. And that means we can't see it! We only know that dark matter exists because we can observe the effect its gravity has on other things that we can see, such as the rotation of some distant galaxies.

But while this time of stretched-out, invisible light could be thought of as the 'dark ages' of the Universe, don't think that nothing is happening! Regions of dark matter are starting to pull each other together, and dragging in ordinary matter as they do so. Think of it like a class of schoolchildren being organised into teams – gradually growing from a bunch of individuals to groups. All the matter in the Universe began **clumping** together thanks to **gravity**, forming trillions of separate clusters.

Yes, gravity is another of the four fundamental forces. Without gravity the Sun would not have started shining and the Earth would not have formed. Gravity is very important to us!

THE FORCE OF ATTRACTION

Gravity is a force that pulls things together. Two heavy objects will attract each other more strongly than two light objects. The pull of gravity also depends on how close or far apart two objects are. The closer they are, the stronger the **gravitational pull** between them will be.

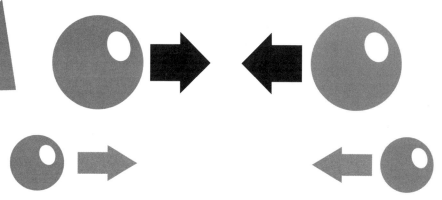

This means that the force of attraction between two objects reduces the further apart they are, but it never completely disappears. In this sense, gravity is the force that connects all matter in the Universe. Gravity stops us from drifting off Planet Earth and into space, and it makes sure that apples on a tree fall conveniently to the ground. It holds the Moon in orbit around the Earth, keeps the other planets in our solar system in orbit around the Sun, and even lets us plan how to send a rocket from Earth to the Moon or to Mars. **Space probes** use the gravity of planets to help boost their speed and adjust their direction as they fly past.

We talk about there being zero gravity in space, but though it seems that way to a floating astronaut, it's not strictly true. On the International Space Station we are most definitely being affected by Earth's gravity, just as we are by the Sun's. The Earth's gravity keeps the ISS in orbit around the Earth, and the Sun's gravity keeps both the Earth and the ISS together in orbit around the Sun. We're even very, very slightly affected by stars on the other side of the galaxy — but the pull from those distant stars is tiny because they are so far away.

Remember those flaws in the early Universe? Imperfections were spread throughout the Universe during cosmic inflation. And that is a good thing, because in a perfect Universe dark matter would not have clumped together under the influence of gravity.

Without these imperfections, there would be no stars in the sky.

So read on to find out how baby stars are born!

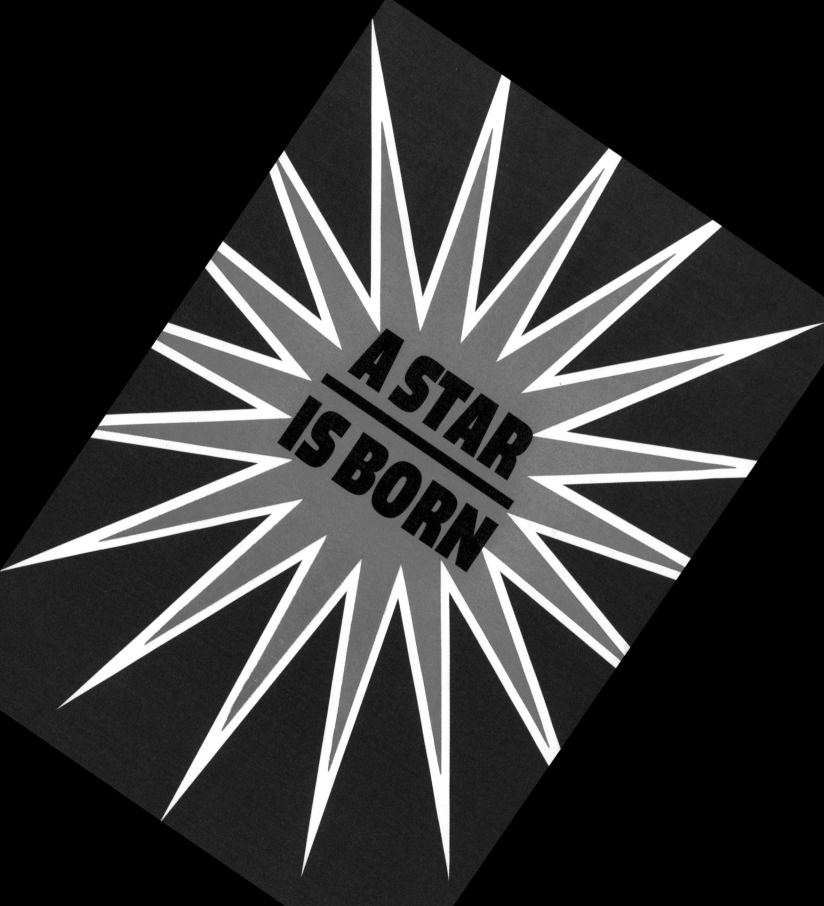

Dear Diary,

180 million years old

I feel much brighter today. You see, I've been suffering from **strange lumps** slowly forming over the past 180 million years or so.

At first, I wasn't too bothered. After all, no one's perfect and what's the odd clump of atoms between friends? But then they started

GROWING, attracting more

atoms and joining together in **ever-bigger groups**.

So, I did what anyone would do when they find a lumpy clump. I gave it a good **SQUEEZE**. And what do you know – it just kind of burst into light and heat. I called it a '**star**'. It was so cool that I started squeezing all over the place, and now I'm simply **awash with starlight**. It's really put me in a party mood!'

THE FIRST STARS . . . OR HOW GRAVITY AND DARK MATTER LIT UP THE UNIVERSE!

After a couple of hundred million years, the force of gravity was slowly getting to work. Do you remember how **the crazy speed of cosmic inflation** meant that some parts of the Universe ended up with more particles than other parts, because the expansion was just a tiny bit uneven? Pockets of more dense matter meant **clouds of gas** slowly clumped together and gravity squashed the atoms closer and closer together. Eventually there was enough heat and pressure in those clouds for nuclear fusion to start. This is where nuclei **fuse together** to make heavier atoms and release energy – including heat and light.

THE COSMIC TUG OF WAR!

The first sparks of nuclear fusion brought light to the Universe once more. At first, massive stars were formed. New stars were forming at a rate ten times faster than we see today.

But it was gravity that was the real headline act this time! It may be a **relatively weak force**, but given enough time, gravity was able to bring billions and billions and billions of hydrogen and helium atoms together, squeezing them into **giant balls of matter**. And since the closer matter is to other bits of matter, the stronger the force of gravity is that keeps pulling them together (as we read in Chapter 3), this process grew ever faster and faster.

But gravity had an enemy – the expanding Universe! As fast as gravity was trying to pull particles of matter together, the expanding Universe was spreading matter thinner and thinner. Gravity would have probably lost this **cosmic tug of war**, and maybe no stars would have ever formed if it hadn't been for that mysterious cloaked stranger the cosmologist mentioned in the previous chapter . . . **dark matter**.*

Remember, we can't see dark matter but we can observe how its gravity affects the things that we can see. Dark matter outnumbers normal matter by about **six parts to one**. So all that dark matter helped to suck in and collapse the giant gas clouds into balls of hydrogen and helium.

As the hydrogen and helium particles were squished tighter and tighter together, the resulting clumps of matter became hotter and hotter. Eventually they became hot enough for nuclear fusion to begin. It's like the spark that starts your campfire burning. The clump starts to burn hydrogen and helium – and it begins to shine.

The first stars were born.

*Dark matter isn't really a cloaked stranger – in real life, you can't see dark matter at all. But that would make a boring picture!

Dear Diary,

200 million years old

Those stars are **WAAAAY** cooler than I first thought. Well, actually they're pretty hot, but you know what I mean . . .

There's some kind of **magic** going on inside them. All I gave them was hydrogen, helium and a tiny bit of lithium, but they've started creating all sorts of other stuff all by themselves!

What show-offs! I kind of like them, though . . .

STAR FACTORIES: THE GIANTS ARE UNLEASHED!

These early stars, called **HOT BLUE GIANTS**, were MASSIVE. 'Giants' because they may have been many hundreds of times BIGGER than the Sun, and 'blue' because, just like a flame, the hotter the star, the bluer it burns.

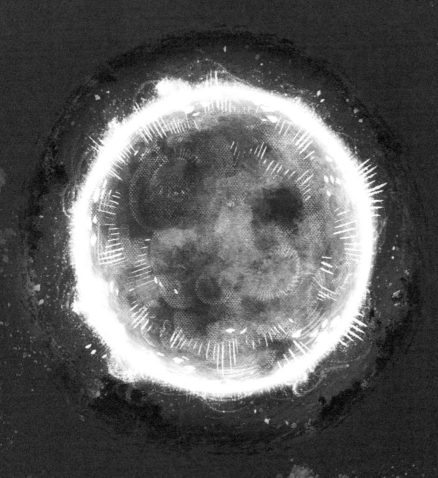

Those hot blue giants were so **HUGE** that the nuclear reactions inside their cores didn't stop at fusing hydrogen into helium. Once they had used up most of the hydrogen, they started crushing helium to a temperature of 100 million degrees Celsius. At this point it began to fuse into **carbon** and **oxygen** – two of the essential elements for life!

You may have thought that these massive stars would live longer – but in fact the opposite is true. The huge size of these early stars meant that gravity was crushing all the atoms in the star closer together. So these **early, massive stars** burned through their fuel at an incredible rate.

Nuclear fusion taking place inside the star releases a lot of energy in the form of heat and light. The heat released during nuclear fusion is keeping the star alive by pushing outwards against the force of gravity that's trying to squash it tightly together. But a massive star needs to burn a massive amount of fuel to maintain this balancing act and stay alive.

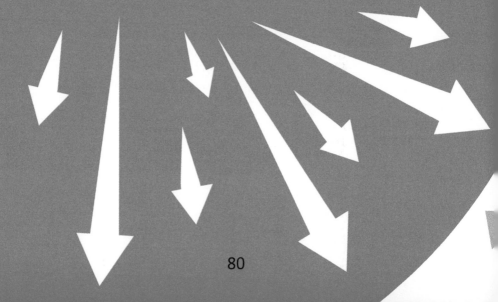

During the time when a star has this balance between gravity pushing in and the pressure from nuclear fusion pushing out, it is known as a 'main sequence' star.

How long does a star live?

Stars spend around 90 per cent of their lifetime in the 'main sequence' phase. The length of time the star is in its balanced main sequence phase depends on its size. Bigger stars burn faster, while smaller stars burn slower and last longer. A star 50 times the mass of the Sun (like a blue giant) might burn through its fuel in as little as a million years.

So, if our Sun was a blue giant, I'm afraid you would not be reading this. However, our Sun is already 5 billion years old and will live on for at least another 5 billion, because it is much smaller than a blue giant and burns more slowly — so we don't need to move anywhere else for a while!

Dear Diary,

201 million years old

My first big stars just kept creating more and more different types of atoms by squashing nuclei together. These bigger atoms are getting heavier and heavier.

Maybe all this new stuff will come in handy one day? I can't help wondering how it's all going to end — something tells me that these giant stars aren't going to just fizzle out and die quietly . . .

STAR FACTORIES

As stars begin to burn up most of the hydrogen and helium that they were using for fuel, things start to change. As the middle of the star – its core – runs out of hydrogen and then helium, it starts collapsing. Gravity suddenly finds its job of squishing easier because there's less pressure pushing outwards from burning hydrogen and helium. The core gets **hotter and hotter** as it gets squashed smaller and smaller by gravity.

The star has already fused hydrogen into helium. When it burns up helium it makes carbon, and then it fuses carbon and helium to make oxygen. As the star gets squashed smaller and hotter it keeps fusing atoms into ever-heavier elements.

Once the temperature reaches **600 million degrees Celsius**, really massive stars are able to fuse carbon into neon, sodium, magnesium and aluminium. At even greater temperatures and pressures, further fusion takes place – creating elements such as silicon, sulphur, argon and calcium, until eventually, in the most massive stars, iron is created.

Our star has now created in its core all the elements that make up **99 per cent of Earth**.

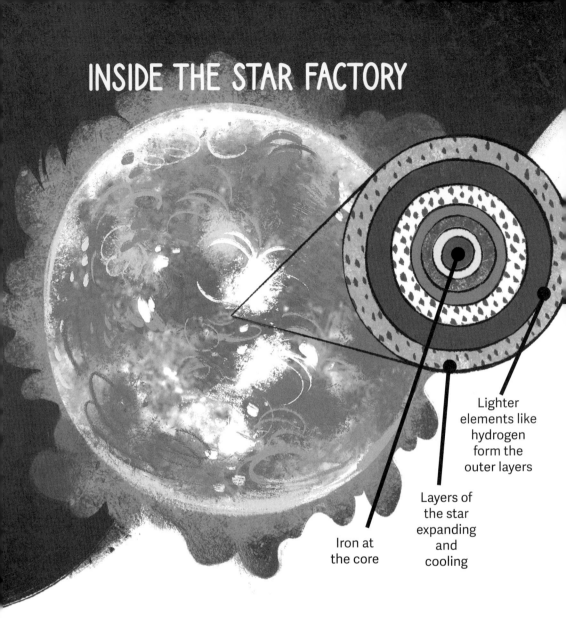

Lighter
elements like
hydrogen
form the
outer layers

Layers of
the star
expanding
and
cooling

Iron at
the core

But while the core is getting **hotter and smaller** with super-massive temperatures and pressures, some **hydrogen** and **helium** remains in the outer layers of the star, still fusing and releasing heat and light. These outer layers of the star start to expand away from the core and the star's surface temperature cools. This also causes its **colour to change**.

As it grows old, a hot blue giant star gets **bigger and bigger**.

Eventually it turns into a giant star we call a **RED SUPERGIANT**.

The biggest stars are a bit like an onion, with layer after layer of heavier elements as you move from the hydrogen at the surface towards the iron at the core. But the buck stops with iron – and it stops with a **BANG . . .**

Why does nuclear fusion in the star stop once it has created iron atoms? The answer has to do with the strong nuclear force you read about in chapter 2. Now turn the page ...

ATOMIC POWER

The strong nuclear force only works over really, *really* tiny distances, like the nucleus of an atom. This force is like a strong elastic band that snaps into place during nuclear fusion to bind the protons in the nucleus tightly together, even though they want to repel each other.

But the nuclei of bigger, heavier atoms, like iron, get bigger too as you add more protons and neutrons. Eventually the nuclei get big enough that the strong nuclear force can't wrap around the whole nucleus. When this happens, **nuclear fusion can't continue**.

Until nuclear fusion in the star is at the point of creating iron, each fusion reaction has **produced energy**. But making atoms heavier than iron uses up more energy than it releases. Nuclear fusion can no longer work. And that means the star has nothing left to push against the gravity crushing down on its core . . .

Dear Diary,

210 million years old

Holy smokes! I was taking a nap around noon and
all of a sudden this

ENORMOUS

bang woke me up.

Those stars I made have taken on a life of their own and now some of
them are blowing up all over the place. It's creating a terrible mess –
there's stuff everywhere. I just hope someone will help me clean up . . .

SHOCKWAVES, COSMIC RAYS AND SUPERNOVAS!

When a massive star fuses iron in its core, that spells the end of its life. With nuclear fusion no longer possible, our star is doomed. Gravity **wins the fight** and the iron core begins to collapse and heat up.

It heats up slowly at first, but when the temperature reaches a crazy **10 BILLION** degrees Celsius it suddenly completely collapses under its own weight. Imagine the inner core of a **MASSIVE** star – about **12,000 kilometres** across – being squeezed to just 20 kilometres in diameter. That's a shorter distance than the narrowest part of the English Channel!

But that's as far as it can go. Gravity squashes the iron atoms in the star's core really fast, as tightly packed as protons and neutrons inside a single atomic nucleus. When it can't be squashed any further it stops with a shuddering jolt. And because it stops so quickly, a **shockwave** starts to move outwards. When this happens, the shockwave going outwards meets the rest of the layers of the core still falling inwards.

When the shockwave meets the outer layers of the star, it sets the scene for something truly spectacular.

It's one of the biggest explosions in the Universe – a **SUPERNOVA**.

As the outrushing blast meets the rest of the core still falling inwards, neutrons are smashed into all the matter so far created by the star. This creates even more new elements. Some particles are accelerated to close to the speed of light, creating **cosmic rays**. These cosmic rays then smash apart heavier nuclei.

When astronauts close their eyes at night, we frequently see flashes of light before falling asleep. These are galactic cosmic rays striking the retina at the back of our eyes. These rays may have been travelling through the Universe for billions of years from a distant supernova before hitting our unsuspecting retinas!

The supernova explosion enables the dying star to give us a few last treats – new elements, some of which are heavier than iron. The resulting massive explosion disperses these elements far and wide.

Many of these elements will be lost to space or swallowed up by new stars forming. But in at least one small corner of the Universe, some of these elements will find themselves coming together to help form a small, rocky planet called **Earth**. And in turn, those elements on Earth will come together to create life.

So if you hear someone say that we are all stardust . . . they're right. We really are.

How big is a supernova explosion?

In January 2016, a cosmic explosion was detected 3.6 billion light years away that flashed 200 times brighter than a normal supernova – or 20 times more brilliant than the 100 billion stars in the Milky Way galaxy combined. It has been calculated that the brightest a supernova can possibly get is 5 trillion times the glare of the Sun. Now that's a pretty good firework!

AFTER THE SUPERNOVA . . . .

While we owe our existence to massive stars
and supernovae forging elements and throwing
them out into space, that is not the end of their
story. Things are about to get heavy around
here, because what some massive stars leave
behind is really quite incredible. Most of the
elements that make up your body have just
been created inside massive stars. But in order
to forge the small amounts of really heavy
elements in your body like iodine, it's going to
take an even bigger punch than a supernova.

Hang on tight as we enter the realm
of neutron stars and . . .

BLACK
HOLES.

BLACK

HOLES

AND OTHER
HEAVY STUFF

Dear Diary,

250 milion years old

Well, that was exciting, wasn't it? It seems you can have **SO MUCH** fun with a bit of hydrogen and helium if you have a few hundred million years to play with!

I thought that when my stars went **BANG**, that was it! The gas, dust and other stuff they leave behind is quite pretty. But just wait till you hear what happened next . . .

WHAT HAPPENS AFTER A SUPERNOVA?

When a massive star explodes into a supernova, it throws out atoms of hydrogen, helium and all the elements that were created in the star by fusion. A cloud of this 'stardust' in space looks incredible and can take many shapes. It is called a **nebula**.

After a supernova explosion, the heavy iron core of the star is left behind. If it's an average-sized core, around 20 kilometres or less across, it will become a **neutron star**. Neutron stars are roughly between 12 to 20 kilometres in diameter, but don't let their size fool you into thinking they're not powerful!

A nebula is sometimes also called a star nursery because gravity can make these clouds clump together to make brand new stars. Our very own Sun came from one of these star nurseries!

95

Which is the nearest star nursery to Earth?

The Orion Nebula – also known as Messier 42 – can be found in the constellation of Orion right here in our galaxy, the Milky Way. It lies approximately 1500 light years from Earth.

Neutron stars have been squashed by gravity until they are incredibly dense. Just one single teaspoonful of neutron star would weigh as much as a mountain on Earth!

The gravitational pull of a neutron star is so extreme that if you were to stand on one, you would weigh about 7 BILLION tonnes!

When the iron core of a massive star collapses, everything gets **squeezed together** super-tightly. So super-tightly that even protons and electrons combine to form neutrons. Indeed, you mostly end up with just a load of neutrons squashed together with no room to move . . . hence the name **neutron star**!

Although neutron stars are quite rare, and space is a pretty big place, they do sometimes find each other thanks to gravity. Neutron stars are **so dense** that they have a mighty gravitational pull on them . . .

STAR DOOM!

When two neutron stars find each other, they start to orbit each other, getting faster and faster as they get closer and closer. Just imagine **two ping-pong balls** being funnelled down a huge, swirling plughole! By the time the neutron stars collide, they're two super-heavy objects both moving at close to **110 million kilometres per hour**.

When neutron stars collide, an enormous burst of neutrons is blasted into the surrounding matter. As neutrons are smashed into other atoms with incredible force, they create new and heavier elements.

Now that's going to cause one CATACLYSMIC BANG!

So, while hydrogen, helium and lithium formed when the Universe first cooled, all the other elements were created by the spectacular deaths of stars, spreading them far and wide through the Universe through colossal explosions.

Without all these elements, **Earth would not exist – and neither would we**.

The elements in space, in the planets, moons, asteroids, comets and even ourselves, were formed long ago by the incredible forces unleashed by the Big Bang and the life cycle of stars. You can see all these elements in the periodic table at the back of this book. The shaded elements can all be found in our own bodies in different amounts. So without the stars, we wouldn't be alive right here and now.

Some elements are more common than others. For instance, gold or uranium are very rare. Because they are hard to get hold of, they become more valuable.

Dear Diary,

300 million years old

Well, I didn't set out to do it on purpose, but thanks to my

idea of stars it looks like I've created an awesome collection of elements. These elements will one day make up . . .

ALL LIVING THINGS!

But it seems that supernovae and neutron stars are not the only things to come from the death of stars . . .

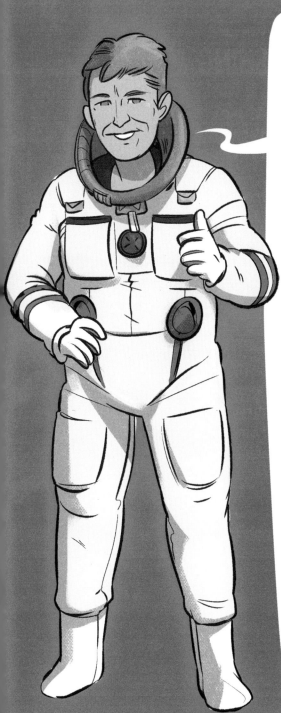

We have seen how huge forces shaped the Universe and created the building blocks needed for life — and for YOU. The story so far has been full of drama and excitement. We've gone from the Big Bang to matter and the first atoms . . . the first light and the whole electromagnetic spectrum . . . the first stars and supernovae making heavier atoms and scattering them through space.

Now, we are ready to get closer to our home address in space — the Milky Way galaxy. But first, let's find out about those mysterious objects in space that lurk at the centre of the Milky Way — and possibly at the centre of all galaxies — terrifying, gravity-sucking

BLACK HOLES!

THE COSMIC VANISHING ACT!

Hugely, enormously **BIG** stars that have a really big iron core go beyond creating a supernova or crushing themselves down into neutron stars. Instead they turn into a **black hole**!

When a really massive star runs out of fuel for nuclear fusion and starts to collapse, a huge amount of mass is being squeezed into a tiny space. Gravity crushes the star down smaller and smaller and smaller, even further than a neutron star, until it becomes a black hole. A black hole's gravity is incredibly strong. So strong that nothing (not even light) can escape – so the star simply seems to **vanish**.

Scientists still don't understand exactly what happens inside a black hole. Things get crushed so far that we can't fathom how **SOOO** much stuff can squeeze into such a tiny space. The laws of physics break down – space and time are squashed by gravity to a point where they become meaningless.

It takes a BIG star, 15–20 times bigger than our Sun, to create a black hole!

We call this point at the centre of a black hole a **singularity**.

 ## How do we detect black holes?

Black holes can't be seen because light can't escape from them – but their gravity sucks gas and dust inside, making a disc around the black hole that can be spotted. The gas molecules in the disc swirl around the black hole so fast that they heat up and give off X-rays. These wavelengths of light can be detected on Earth – another sure giveaway that there's a black hole hiding out there!

ANATOMY OF A BLACK HOLE

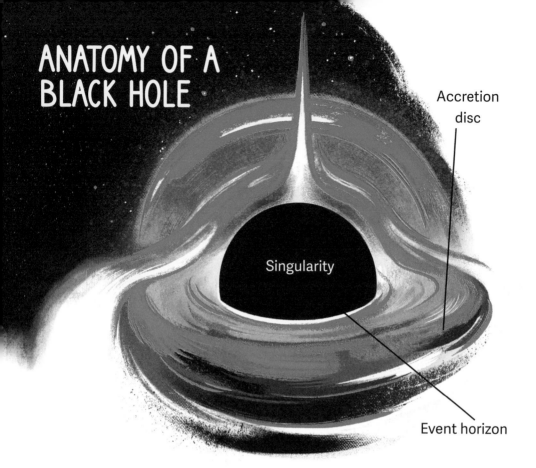

Accretion disc

Singularity

Event horizon

THE POINT OF NO RETURN

NOTHING can escape the gravitational pull of a black hole. It's like being sucked into a colossal whirlpool and no matter how hard you swim, you cannot fight the current. Nothing can! And black holes have enormous appetites. They begin to suck up all matter in their vicinity and grow bigger. Not everything can get in all at once and, just like **water trying to rush down a plughole**, a spiralling disc of gas, dust and debris called the accretion disc forms around the black hole, waiting its turn to be sucked inside!

The point at which even light is sucked into the black hole is called **the event horizon**.

But some black holes are simply unstoppable. As they get bigger and bigger they suck in nearby stars, stripping them of their layers of gas and material, and growing ever larger. And, just like neutron stars, black holes can collide too, becoming **SUPERMASSIVE BLACK HOLES**.

At the heart of our Milky Way galaxy is a supermassive black hole called Sagittarius A*, which is about 4 MILLION times the mass of the Sun!

But Sagittarius A* is just a pinprick compared to the distant TON 618, a black hole that weighs in at 66 BILLION times the mass of the Sun!

What would happen if you fell into a black hole?

Let's get the bad news out of the way first, because it's not going to end well! Stray too close to a black hole and first you'll start to notice things looking a bit distorted as gravity begins to warp the world around you. As you get pulled past the event horizon, there's no escape. The immense gravitational forces will stretch you out like a piece of spaghetti, while other bits of you might get shredded to pieces. All in all – OUCH, you'd end up a bit of a Bolognese. Better steer clear of black holes!

So, now we know just what stars can do in their dying days. Their afterlife in the Universe is **spectacular** and can have huge effects – whether they create elements to be flung through space or relentlessly suck in all matter around them.

There's still a lot to discover about black holes and why they often turn up in the centre of galaxies . . . so read on to find out more about this galactic mystery!

6

GROWING
A
GALAXY

Dear Diary,

650 million years old

When you're as

crazy

big

as I am,

it's easy to get confused. Now I'm not exactly sure if galaxies spring up around supermassive black holes or if the galaxies were there first . . .

HOW GALAXIES GROW

We know that galaxies are a collection of stars, gas, dust and dark matter – all held together by our old friend gravity. But it's difficult for scientists to know exactly how they first formed.

In the early Universe, galaxies are thought to have begun as small clouds of stars, gas and dust. **Gravity** causes stars to group together, swirling, spinning and colliding, and gravity also causes more stars to form by clumping gas and dust particles together in space.

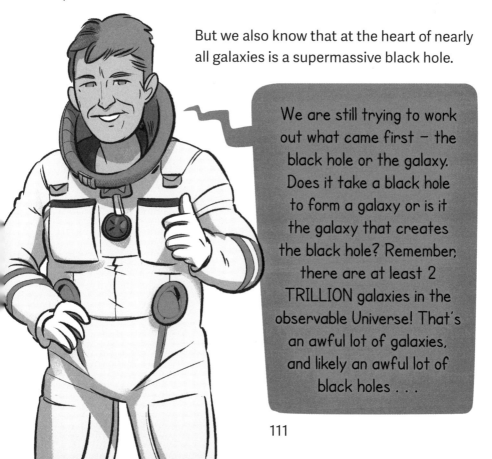

But we also know that at the heart of nearly all galaxies is a supermassive black hole.

We are still trying to work out what came first – the black hole or the galaxy. Does it take a black hole to form a galaxy or is it the galaxy that creates the black hole? Remember, there are at least 2 TRILLION galaxies in the observable Universe! That's an awful lot of galaxies, and likely an awful lot of black holes . . .

The observable Universe is simply how much of the Universe we can see through our most powerful telescopes. Light takes time to travel. The Universe is so immense that the light from distant stars may take billions of years to reach us. And since the Universe is expanding as we speak, we will NEVER get to see all of it!

It is possible that galaxies and black holes both **evolved together**, with a young galaxy helping to feed a newly formed black hole which, in turn, draws in more dust, gas and stars. Cosmologists are still trying to find the answer to this – and luckily there is a lot of evidence out there . . .

The strange thing is, even the most **GIGANTIC** supermassive black holes are relatively tiny compared to the mass of an entire galaxy. Black holes can be supermassive, but galaxies gather more and more stars and become even bigger. So even if a galaxy and its black hole start out together, at some point the galaxy becomes a really, really big brother. Although the supermassive black hole at the centre of the Milky Way has the mass of some 4 million Suns, the combined mass of the galaxy is around a colossal **1.5 TRILLION** Suns.

The Plough

Remember, stars move and change and die over time. In the far far future, the star patterns in the night sky that we currently recognise – known as constellations – will look very different or disappear altogether. New ones will have taken their place. One of the easiest to spot is Ursa Major, the Great Bear, because it contains the stars in the shape of what we call the Plough, or Big Dipper. Don't worry, you'll still be able to recognise the Plough for many thousands of years!

DAZZLING DISTANCES

It's pretty incredible to think that the mass of the whole galaxy is about the same as 1.5 trillion Suns. But at a galactic level, *all* the figures are mind blowing!

For instance, our galaxy stretches about 946,000,000,000,000,000 kilometres from one side to the other. That's **a lot of zeros** to handle when you're doing calculations!

Because space is so incredibly huge, we usually measure distances in larger, easier units known as **light years**. A light year isn't a measure of time. It's simply a measure of the distance light travels in an Earth year.

Light is the speediest thing in the Universe. It travels at 299,792 kilometres per second. One light year is the distance a photon of light can travel in 365 days, which is about 9.46 trillion kilometres. Would you rather say 1 light year or 9,460,000,000,000 kilometres?

It's much clearer to calculate such vast distances in light years (or even light days, light hours or light minutes) than in kilometres.

How long does the Sun's light take to reach Earth?

It takes **8 minutes and 20 seconds** for light to travel from the surface of the Sun to Earth – a distance of **147,560,000 kilometres.** It takes light about **4.24 years** to get from the Sun to our nearest star, called Proxima Centauri.

Again, an Earth year is a measure of time, while a light year is a measure of distance. Obviously it takes light one year to travel a distance of **one light year!**

Dear Diary,

700 million years old

My galaxies are beautiful and come in a glorious array of shapes and sizes, but when they bump into each other, boy, there's a lot of pushing and shoving! After that, they sometimes decide to hang out or to draw even closer together . . .

Good news is, I'm definitely feeling more peaceful than I used to!

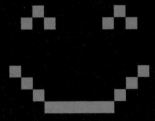

WHAT HAPPENS WHEN WHOLE GALAXIES COLLIDE?

When the first galaxies formed, our Universe was a lot smaller than it is today. But since gravity always brings things together, at some point they're going to **bump** into each other. Luckily, unlike an explosive neutron-star collision, when galaxies 'collide' it's more like two large crowds of people joining together, with everyone jostling around, trying to find some space to get comfy again.

In the far future, our galaxy, the Milky Way, will actually merge with our galactic neighbour, Andromeda. But don't rush to pack your bags – it won't happen for about another 4.5 billion years!

Do you remember Planet Earth's 'address' on page 4? That shows you how gravity has drawn galaxies together into clusters . . . and then superclusters!

SPOTTING SUPERCLUSTERS

As telescopes and computers become more powerful, they help us to learn more about what's happening in space around us.

Our **Milky Way galaxy** resides in the Local Group together with two other large spiral galaxies – **Andromeda** and **Triangulum** – and over 80 other medium-sized and small galaxies spread over a few million light years.

But don't forget the rest of our address in space. Like a neighbourhood inside a larger city, our Local Group is part of the **Virgo Supercluster**, which contains at least 100 groups of galaxies in an area of space 110 million light years across. Is your mind blown yet, or are you ready for more? Because the Virgo Supercluster itself is in turn part of the **EVEN BIGGER Laniakea Supercluster**, containing at least 100,000 other galaxies in an area of space about **520 million light years across**.

GALACTIC SHAPES

Not all galaxies are the same. We sort them into different types, depending on their shape.

The Milky Way is a spiral galaxy! The Earth orbits the Sun in the middle of one of its spiral arms.

A spiral galaxy bulges in the middle and has arms that spiral around the centre of the galaxy.

An elliptical galaxy is shaped like an oval. It also has a bulge in the middle, but it doesn't have any spiral arms and can be stretched quite thin and long.

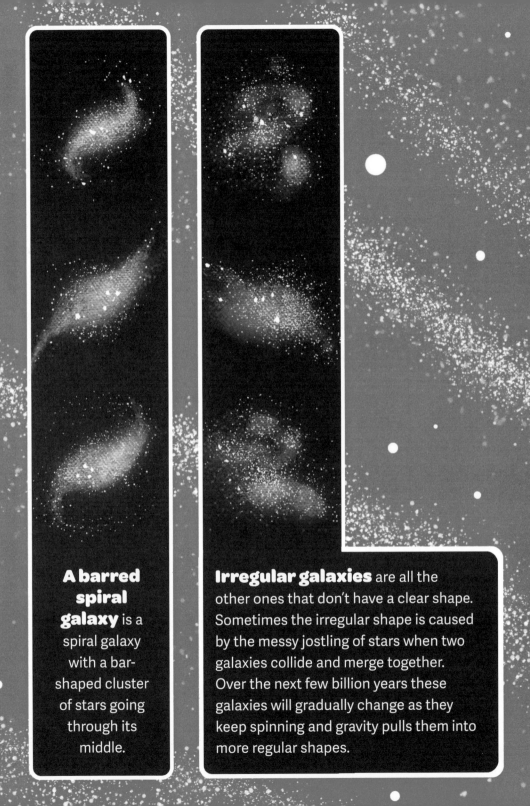

A barred spiral galaxy is a spiral galaxy with a bar-shaped cluster of stars going through its middle.

Irregular galaxies are all the other ones that don't have a clear shape. Sometimes the irregular shape is caused by the messy jostling of stars when two galaxies collide and merge together. Over the next few billion years these galaxies will gradually change as they keep spinning and gravity pulls them into more regular shapes.

HOW DID THE MILKY WAY GET ITS NAME?

It's thought that the Milky Way gets its name from an ancient Greek myth about the goddess Hera, who sprayed milk across the sky in a **wide milky circle**. The ancient Greek for milk was **'gala'**, which is how we got the name 'galaxy'.

Most galaxies are between **10 and 13.6 billion years old**. Astronomers use several methods to estimate the age of a galaxy, for example by measuring **radioactive elements** or the **cooling of stars**. Our own Milky Way is thought to contain some of the oldest stars in the Universe.

The Milky Way formed much like any other galaxy, gathering clouds of gas and dust, and sucking in smaller dwarf galaxies.

In 2018, astronomers reported the discovery of a tiny star in our own Milky Way made almost entirely of materials released from the Big Bang. It is 13.5 billion years old and possibly one of the very first stars! Astronomers have given it the exciting name of 2MASS J18082002-5104378 B. Snappy! Do you have any more interesting suggestions?

Some experts believe that nearly half the matter in the Milky Way has been pulled in from other galaxies.

After a few billion years, the Milky Way had grown large enough for gravity to start spinning it around its centre. As it picked up speed, the ball of gas and matter started to flatten out into a disc, and the Milky Way ended up in the familiar spiral shape that we see today.

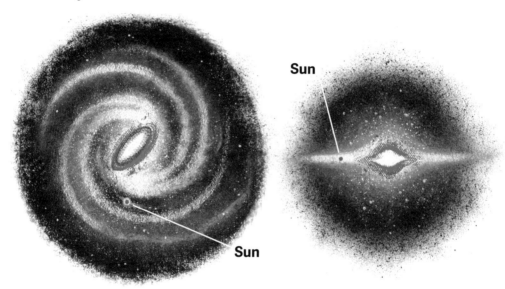

Sun

Sun

A HEAVENLY HOST OF STARS

Galaxies are filled with stars of all different kinds. For instance, our Sun is a **yellow dwarf star**. It is certainly not one of the biggest stars around, but it is a good size and burns quite brightly. In about 5 billion years it will expand into a red giant star.

Our Milky Way is about 100,000 light years wide but only 1,000 light years deep. It's estimated to contain between 100 and 400 BILLION stars.

The most common type of stars are **red dwarfs**. These are smaller than the Sun and make up about 75 per cent of all stars in the Universe. Red and yellow dwarfs are not massive enough to fuse iron in their core and go out with a COLOSSAL BANG like the Supernova (see page 95). Instead, they will collapse to become **white dwarfs**, eventually cooling and ending their lives as **black dwarfs**.

Just to add to the variety, there are brown dwarfs out there in space, too. Brown dwarfs are massive gas giants that weren't large enough to ignite hydrogen fusion and become stars. But they're pretty impressive to look at, anyway!

	Brown dwarf	Red dwarf	Yellow dwarf (Sun-like)	Supergiant
MASS	0.08 x Sun	0.2 x Sun	1 x Sun	20 x Sun
TEMPERATURE (SURFACE)	1,000 degrees Celsius	3,000 degrees Celsius	5,000 degrees Celsius	12,000 degrees Celsius
LIFE EXPECTANCY		10 trillion years	10 billion years	5 million years

In case you're wondering how there can be enough gas to ignite all the stars that we see in the Universe, only 2 per cent of the hydrogen and helium in the galaxy has been transformed into other elements. There's still plenty of hydrogen and helium left to make new stars.

Dear Diary,

9.24 billion years old

Quick fuel check . . .

98 per cent of my gases remaining.

Happy days!

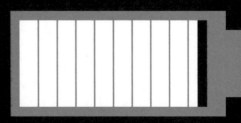

THE PLANETARY NEBULA (THAT ISN'T A PLANET)

Yellow dwarf stars like our Sun eventually become red giants. They aren't big enough to explode as a supernova, but they can still have enough energy to push out a shell of glowing gas and plasma at the end of their life. This is called a **planetary nebula**. Don't be confused by the name – stars cannot become planets! But the shape of the nebula looked like a planet to early astronomers.

In around 5 billion years, our
Sun will turn into a red giant, and
then its outer layers of gas will expand
and create a planetary nebula.

It should be quite a sight! Perhaps one of
your descendents will be watching when it
happens? Because, by then, the human race
will have moved on to new worlds . . .

Dear Diary,

9.2 billion years old

That's the funny thing about stars. Once they've burned into life, they sometimes gather a group of planets that spin around them. And if those planets are not too close to their star and not too far away, something very special can happen: LIFE.

I currently have this one star in a spiral arm of the Milky Way, 27,000 light years from the galactic centre. Do you know what? I've got a good feeling about it . . .

THE BIRTH OF OUR SUN

We already know that when stars are born, gravity goes to work on clouds of dust and gas, crushing them down until **nuclear fusion** sparks a new star into light.

Our Sun is a much smaller star than some of the **first supergiants** of the early Universe. As a later generation star, it was born from lots of elements besides just hydrogen and helium, and they can't help but cool a star as it is forming. So, rather than becoming a massive, hot and fast-burning star, the Sun instead became a yellow dwarf, burning at a much steadier rate, with a surface temperature of about **5,500 degrees Celsius**.

Our Sun is about halfway through its **10-billion-year lifespan**, so about 5 billion years old. That's A LOT of birthday candles.

The Sun's diameter is about 109 times wider than the Earth. But its mass is about 330,000 times that of the Earth. Because the Sun has much more mass than the Earth, the Sun's gravity pulls on the Earth much more strongly than the Earth's gravity pulls on the Sun. That's why the Earth orbits the Sun and not the other way around.

How does the Sun give energy to Earth?

In its core right now, the Sun is fusing about 600 million tons of hydrogen into helium every second. This energy can take between 10,000 and 170,000 years to escape the core as light and heat.

Sunlight supports almost all life on Earth. Plants use photosynthesis to turn sunlight and carbon dioxide into energy and also to provide oxygen for us to breathe. Solar power is a renewable source of energy that we can use as an alternative to coal or gas power. The Sun produces much more energy than we actually need. Where would we be without it? We would be a frozen rock spinning aimlessly through outer space! Not a lot of fun . . .

It takes around 250 MILLION years for the Sun to complete ONE orbit of the Milky Way galaxy's centre. This is known as a cosmic year!

Just imagine the young Sun billions of years ago, burning brightly. It had a disc of hot gas, metals, rocks and dust grains **swirling around it**.

Luckily for us, from that dusty debris, whole other worlds would form and circle the Sun. Among them was our own planet . . .

Dear Diary,

9.26 billion years old

My head is spinning! I have more than a billion trillion stars burning inside me, as well as all the rocky or gassy substances travelling about them. Honestly, they take so long to form, and sometimes they break apart again, or comets and meteors smash into them.

It really is a **messy business**.

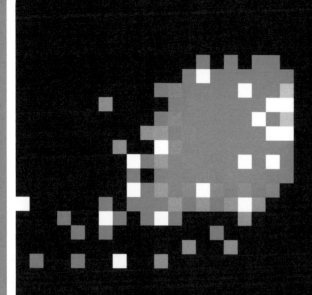

But then, so is the creation of life, I guess - and some of the rockier planets look **ripe** for something **amazing** to take place . . .

THE EARLY SOLAR SYSTEM

There are eight planets in our solar system – **Mercury**, **Venus**, **Earth**, **Mars**, **Jupiter**, **Saturn**, **Uranus** and **Neptune**. We used to think of **Pluto** as a planet but since 2006 it's been called a **dwarf planet**. The 'official' dwarf planets beyond Pluto are **Makemake**, **Haumea** and **Eris** but there are many other small and distant worlds at the reaches of the solar system.

The early solar system was very different to the stable, orderly arrangement of planets that we know today. When the Sun first formed, there was still lots of leftover gas and dust swirling around it in a massive disc.

In the hot zone, closest to the Sun, only the heavier elements could condense into solid matter. Lighter elements like hydrogen, helium and oxygen were swept further away from the Sun by the **solar wind**. Oxygen loves to bond with other elements, and with so much hydrogen around it was only natural that these two elements would get together and begin to form water molecules.

We mentioned the solar wind — but it's really more of a solar hurricane! The intense heat and energy of the Sun hurls tiny particles out into space at incredible speeds, blowing atoms of different elements with them, clear across the solar system.

PLANETS FORM S-L-O-W-L-Y

Have you ever rolled a snowball down a hill to make a huge snowman? Well, making a planet begins in a similar way – by starting out very small and gradually accumulating stuff to grow bigger and bigger.

Throughout the solar system, gravity turned ice and dust and dirt into solid lumps which very slowly joined with others to become **planetesimals** – small, rocky objects. And we mean ve-r-r-r-y slowly. It took about ten thousand years for clumps of ice and dust in our solar system to become just the size of sugar cubes! It would take at least another 10 MILLION years before these planetesimals clumped together like toy building bricks to eventually build rocky planets. In fact, it took about a thousand times longer to assemble the Earth than it did to form the Sun.

The Earth formed about **4.5 billion years ago**.

Leftover planetesimals remain in the solar system today as lumpy asteroids or comets!

Nearer the Sun, the planetesimals contained mostly rocky and metallic elements. Further out, where the disc of gas and dust was colder, some planetesimals contained lighter gassy elements – such as frozen hydrogen, helium and water ice.

This explains the make-up of our solar system – there are smaller rocky planets closer to the Sun like Earth and Mars, while the gas giants like Jupiter and Saturn formed further out.

As our young Earth slowly grew in size, the dust, rock, ice and other elements were all squeezed together under ever-increasing gravity.

Much like in the case of a star, once you start crushing things together, they heat up. There was also a lot of heat generated by collisions as lumps of rock and other planetesimals smashed into Earth. With so much heat being generated, our early Earth soon became a ball of molten rock.

Why does the Earth have seasons?

Some of these rock and planetesimal collisions were big enough to knock the Earth slightly sideways! This meant that the Earth has ended up spinning with a slight tilt.

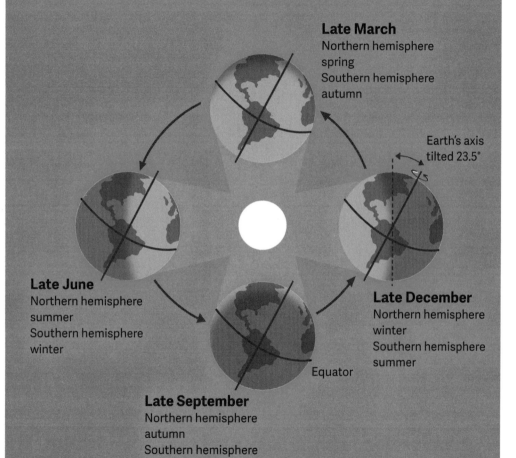

Late March
Northern hemisphere spring
Southern hemisphere autumn

Earth's axis tilted 23.5°

Late June
Northern hemisphere summer
Southern hemisphere winter

Late December
Northern hemisphere winter
Southern hemisphere summer

Equator

Late September
Northern hemisphere autumn
Southern hemisphere spring

Without the tilt we would have no seasons. The tilt of the Earth means that in the part of Earth's orbit where its axis points more towards the Sun, that hemisphere is in summer and the other hemisphere that points more away from the Sun is in winter.

SHOOT FOR THE MOON!

While many planetesimals joined together to make planets like Mercury, Venus, Earth and Mars, other planetesimals were still hurtling free through space like giant snooker balls. Most astronomers believe that one such planetesimal **crashed into the Earth hard**, when the Earth was very young.

The crash threw bits of the Earth's crust **into space**, and this material orbited the Earth together with some of the broken bits of the planetesimal itself. Over the centuries to come, these materials clumped together with the help of gravity to form the Moon.

When the Moon was new it was about **fifteen times** closer to the Earth. At that time, the Earth's day was much shorter – just **six hours long**! It's thought that the Moon may even have helped create the right conditions for life to form . . .

Dear Diary,

9.39 billion years old

My rocky planets and gassy planets are remarkable. But it's really quite something when I spot a planet with liquid water. All sorts of **miraculous** things can happen when you've got water going on . . .

THIRD ROCK FROM THE SUN

How did the Earth turn from a ball of molten rock into a beautiful blue planet with oceans?

Some of the planetesimals that clumped together to form the Earth contained the ingredients of water: hydrogen and oxygen that were bound up with minerals in these rocks. As the molten ball of rock that was the early Earth cooled, it developed a solid crust – like a thick skin over a hot custard. But molten rock – or magma – underneath the crust got thrown up sometimes by erupting volcanoes. That released the hydrogen and oxygen in the magma into the atmosphere. Hydrogen and oxygen mixed to form water molecules, which eventually fell to Earth as rain.

Water also came to Earth from the chaotic early solar system, carried by meteors and comets hitting the Earth.

SPACE ROCKS! ASTEROIDS, METEORS AND COMETS

Asteroids, meteors and comets helped create the oceans by bringing more oxygen and hydrogen to the Earth. But what are they and where did they come from?

Basically, all these things are leftover planetesimals. There are millions of comets and asteroids orbiting the Sun. These days we can find asteroids in two main places in the solar system. The asteroid belt is a region in the solar system between Mars and Jupiter that contains many planetesimals. They are much, much smaller than planets; most asteroids are between 1 metres and 5 kilometres across. The two biggest asteroids in the asteroid belt – Vesta and Pallas – are each larger than 500 kilometres across. That's about the distance from London to Edinburgh.

The biggest asteroid in the belt used to be Ceres, at 939 kilometres across – but in 2006 Ceres was promoted to 'dwarf planet' status, alongside Pluto, Eris, Haumea and Makemake, so now Vesta takes the prize at 525 kilometres!

Sun

Mercury, Venus, Earth, Mars

Asteroid belt

Kuiper Belt

Jupiter, Saturn, Uranus, Neptune – the gas giants

OUR SOLAR SYSTEM

The **Kuiper Belt** (named after the astronomer who discovered it) is another doughnut-shaped region of the solar system that starts just beyond the orbit of Neptune. The asteroids and comets in this region contain more ice than those closer to the Sun, because this far out, space is much colder. Remember how gravity pulls on objects even when they are separated from each other? **The pull is stronger from larger objects**. Sometimes the gravitational pull from planets is enough to affect the orbits of icy asteroids in the Kuiper Belt and send them into different orbits – sometimes closer to the Sun.

Very small asteroids, less than a metre across, are usually called **meteoroids**. Sometimes a meteoroid will enter Earth's atmosphere and will burn up brightly due to friction with the air. When that happens it's called a meteor and we will see it as a streak of light in the night sky – **a shooting star**. But if a meteor doesn't burn up completely and manages to get all the way to the ground we call it a meteorite. The words meteoroid, meteor and meteorite all come from a Greek word meaning 'high in the air'.

COLD COMETS

Comets are sometimes nicknamed **'dirty snowballs'** because they contain ice as well as rock – not just water ice but frozen carbon dioxide, methane and other gases.

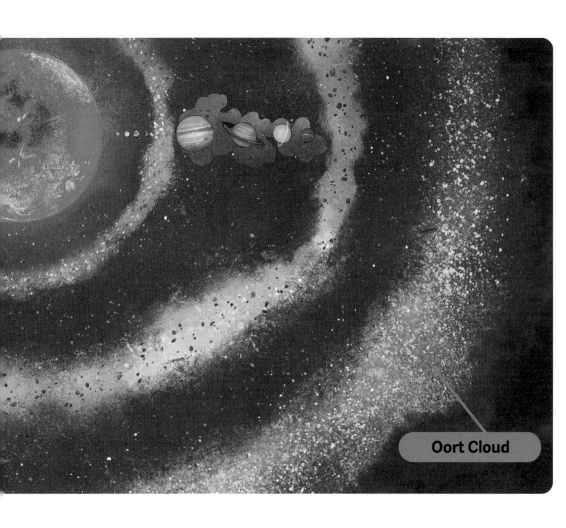

Oort Cloud

Comets that travel round the Sun every 200 years or less are called **short-period comets**. Comets that take longer than 200 years to travel round the Sun are called **long-period comets**. Long-period comets are believed to start out from an area called the **Oort Cloud**, a region shaped like a giant spherical shell that is further out than anything else in the whole solar system.

Sometimes the orbits of comets bring them close enough to the Sun to start to warm up. When they warm up, the ice in the comet starts to **vaporise** back into gases and the comet develops a tail of gas and dust that we can sometimes see from Earth. The solar wind strips tiny amounts of ice and dust from the comet's surface, and as the comet approaches the Sun, the solar wind always blows the comet's tail behind it. However, as the comet travels away from the Sun, the **solar wind** blows the comet's tail in front of it – so the tail is always pointing outwards, away from the Sun!

Halley's Comet is probably the most famous comet. It is a short-period comet, orbiting the inner solar system every 75 years. The last time it was near Earth was in 1986 and the next time will be in 2061.

Why do some planets have rings?

In our solar system, four of the planets – Jupiter, Saturn, Uranus and Neptune – are gas giants made mostly from hydrogen and helium, with small rocky cores. Each of these worlds has rings around it. Saturn's rings are easy to see even with a basic telescope, but the rings around Jupiter, Uranus and Neptune are dark and faint and hard to spot.

These rings look solid from a distance, but they're actually composed of – you guessed it – planetesimals! Billions of pieces of rock, dust and ice that range from tiny specks to lumps the size of a car – or even a house – are swirling around the planet.

This rock, dust and ice is left over from when the gas giant first formed; it is too far away to get squashed by gravity into the rest of the planet but still close enough to stay in orbit. A ring can also be created if a large moon is pulled too close to the planet by gravity and then breaks apart; the pieces stay in orbit and spread out to form a ring. But it also works the other way round. Brand new moons can form from rocks and dust in a planet's rings as gravity pulls some of this matter together into larger clumps.

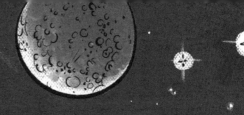

OUTSIDERS: THE EXOPLANETS

The Earth and other planets in our solar system all orbit around our Sun. But many other stars have planets revolving around them. We call them **exoplanets** because exo means **'outside'**, and these exoplanets live outside our solar system. Astronomers give them funny-sounding names that are usually based on whichever star they orbit, for example Gamma Cephei Ab or Kepler 186f.

Planets come in lots of different sizes and colours. Some are small and rocky, like **reddy-orange Mars**, and some are huge and gassy, like **beige-striped Jupiter**. Some of these exoplanets seem similar to Earth and orbit around yellow dwarf stars like our Sun, which is very exciting.

We haven't found life on other planets yet, but we keep looking! And knowing that life is rare reminds us that the abundance of it here on Earth is special and precious. We're moving on fast, so buckle up, because now we're going to take a look at **just how precious life on Earth really is**...

8

COMING
TO LIFE

Dear Diary,

10 billion years old

Today I finally created a living cell on a small rocky planet called Earth.
That's right – **LIFE** has begun on the little blue and green marble
orbiting that average star in that large spiral galaxy – and it looks like
it's going to be a pretty comfortable place for life to exist. It's just
the perfect distance from its sun. Not too cold, not too hot, plenty of
water. Living things ought to flourish here! Who knows what this might
lead to . . .

THE SMALLEST UNIT OF LIFE

The smallest living thing that can exist on its own is a cell. Cells are really small; so small that they can only be seen with a microscope. They look a bit like a tiny sack of fluid. The walls of the sack are called the cell membrane, the fluid inside is called cytoplasm. Inside are the 'internal organs' of the cell – called **organelles**.

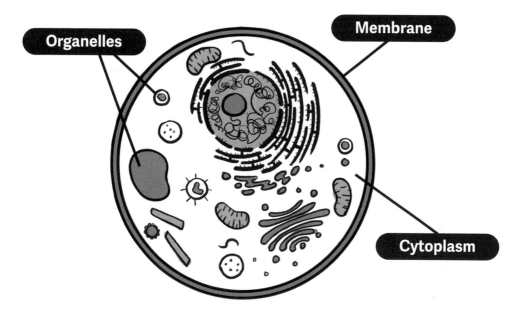

Some organisms are just a single cell – like bacteria. Others are made of many cells working together. A leaf might have **20,000 to 130,000 cells**, depending on its size. The human body meanwhile has over **40 trillion cells**!

WHY WARMTH AND WETNESS WERE ~~WITAL~~ VITAL!

How did life on Earth actually begin? Where did the first cells come from? Where did all the different types of living things – including plants, animals, fungi and even bacteria – come from?

And why is there life on Earth but not on places like **the Moon** or on **Mars**? The difference has to do with Earth's temperature and its oceans. Warmth and water are both essential to the development of life on Earth.

Why is this so? The processes of life – like changing food into energy – involve chemical reactions where atoms in one substance are rearranged to make new products.

Water is great at dissolving other substances and making these important chemical reactions possible. It can also help transport **important nutrients** through a living thing. But it has to be liquid water; ice can't do the job and nor can steam. So the planet's temperature is vital. **If it's too cold or too hot** for liquid water to exist, life won't exist either.

Remember, when the Earth first formed it was a **molten ball of rock** – far too hot for liquid water to exist. As the Earth cooled down, volcanic eruptions and planetesimals hitting the Earth released water into the atmosphere, which eventually formed the oceans.

Once the Earth had its own oceans, a fairly steady temperature was needed for life to first develop there. Luckily, the Moon was around to help with this!

Firstly, the way the Moon orbits the Earth stops it from **wobbling** around too much and keeps the seasons regular (see page 145). If the tilt of the Earth grew more extreme, the climate would be much less stable – and the Earth needs stable conditions for life to arise. Secondly, the Moon causes the tides in Earth's oceans, and this celestial stirring of the water may have actually helped life to grow!

LIFE IN THE (COSMIC) SLOW LANE!

When life emerged on Earth, it wasn't with the speed and explosive drama of the Big Bang! The evolution of life took millions of years; looking back, cosmologists agree that it's not always easy to work out the exact order of things . . .

Evolution is basically the way something develops and adapts and changes over time. Sometimes over a loooooong time! Polar bears have thick white fur, but long ago they used to be brown! Over time, the common brown bear evolved into the polar bear, and its fur colour gradually changed over many generations from brown to white — just the right colour to let it blend in with its snowy environment.

How many different species live on Earth?

There are so many plant and animal species living on Planet Earth that it makes them difficult to count, but current estimates are between 8 million and all the way up to a trillion! Some species live in habitats that we can't explore easily (such as deep trenches in the ocean), some are micro-organisms that are too small to see, are difficult to identify, or live inside other species!

Dear Diary,

10.1 billion years old

Perhaps the small blue-green marble planet could write its own diary, since so many things are happening there! It's so exciting seeing what I've set in motion with sunlight, water and a bunch of raw materials . . . Ah, I remember when that little planet was just a bunch of rocks clumping together. Doesn't time fly?

HOW DID IT ALL BEGIN?

There are different theories about how life on Earth began billions of years ago.

In the late 1800s some scientists thought that organic molecules or bacteria fell to Earth from space (via comets, asteroids and so on), and that these molecules eventually led to life developing on Earth. This idea is known as **'panspermia'**. However, scientists have not found any evidence of bacteria falling to Earth from space. There are no traces of bacteria on Moon rocks either – surely some would have landed on our nearest neighbour, as well as on us, if this bacteria did come from space?

In the 1920s, scientists suggested that, around **4.5 billion years** ago, oceans were much warmer than they are now and contained a mixture of chemicals including methane, ammonia and lots of carbon-based chemicals. The first life formed in this mixture, which became popularly known as **'primordial soup'**.

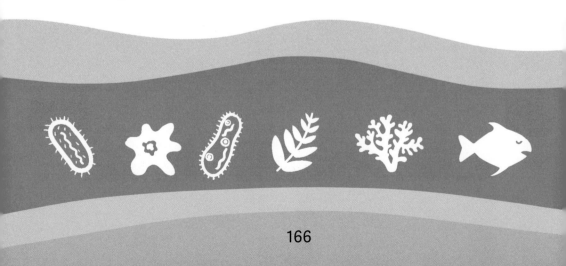

In the 1950s, scientists proved that lightning could cause organic molecules to form from a mix of chemicals that might have come from Earth's early oceans. This theory suggests that the first sparks of life were created by chance from a lucky lightning strike!

Another possibility is that life began thanks to holes or vents deep in the ocean that spurt out super-heated water (up to 400 degrees Celsius) from deep down in the Earth's crust. This water contains chemicals, including sulphides, that create an underwater 'black smoke' effect when they mix with cold ocean water. Energy from the heat and from different chemical reactions may have created the first traces of life in the form of organic molecules – and eventually cells that would create the first marine life.

It has taken billions of years and countless changes and steps in evolution to make all the different types of life on Earth possible, but most scientists now agree that it all started from the very first single-celled organism around **3.8 billion years ago**. Just think – if you could trace your family tree right back to the start, you might find your cousin was a bacterium!

ALL THINGS BRIGHT

A TIMELINE OF LIFE ON EARTH

How did that first single-celled organism evolve into all the different species of life we know about today? Life has changed so much over billions of years, and the Earth has changed too. Let's look at a timeline of life on Earth . . .

4.5 billion years ago: Planet Earth is formed!x

2.4 billion years ago: Early single-celled bacteria in the oceans convert sunlight into energy and produce oxygen as a waste product. Gradually, the amount of oxygen builds . . .

3.8 billion years ago: Earth's atmosphere is mostly carbon dioxide and other gases like nitrogen and methane.

2.3 billion years ago: Earth freezes over for millions of years. Life is on hold.

AND BEAUTIFUL

1.5 billion years ago: Single-celled organisms evolve into three separate groups – the distant ancestors of today's plants, fungi and animals.

770 million years ago: Earth freezes over again.

400 million years ago: Insects evolve. Woody plants start growing, ancestors of the first trees.

900 million years ago: Creatures with many cells appear.

500 million years ago: The first tiny creatures appear on land.

397 million years ago: The first four-legged animals evolve.

250 million years ago: Dinosaurs dominate the Earth, while mammals are small and timid.

150 million years ago: The first birds evolve.

340 million years ago: Amphibians (like frogs and toads) evolve.

180 million years ago: Mammals split into two groups – those that lay eggs and those that give birth to live young.

130 million years ago: The first flowers evolve.

5 million years ago: The first human ancestors evolve.

Today: YOU – a newly evolved human – are reading about how life evolved on your planet!

65 million years ago: Asteroid hits Earth and the dinosaurs become extinct. Birds and mammals survive.

300,000 years ago: Modern humans emerge on the scene.

What kind of life can exist in really harsh conditions?

Tardigrades – also known as water bears – are tiny eight-legged creatures that are about half a millimetre long. They evolved about 600 million years ago and are still around today.

They are amazingly tough. They can survive in extreme heat and cold, high or low pressures, and even without air or water. When conditions are particularly harsh they go into a sort of hibernation and can survive without food or water for an amazing 30 years. Tardigrades have even survived spending 10 days in the vacuum of space! We can learn more about how life survives in different environments by studying tardigrades.

CAN ANYTHING GROW IN SPACE?

On the International Space Station, many plants have been grown successfully – they help astronauts feel more connected to their world, look beautiful and can also taste delicious! And it seems that seeds do not suffer any consequences from the effects of space travel – like vibrations while taking off, temperature changes, **cosmic rays** and **microgravity**. In 1971, astronauts on board Apollo 14 brought a variety of tree seeds on their mission. These seeds circled the Moon with the astronauts and still grew when planted back on Earth, where they are known as **Moon Trees**.

In 2016, I led an experiment with over 600,000 schoolchildren to find out if rocket seeds taken into space for six months would grow the same as regular rocket seeds. The space seeds grew less well than the Earth seeds – but only very slightly. This means that in future, astronauts may end up munching on rocket in our rockets!

IS THERE LIFE ON OTHER WORLDS?

Each planet has a unique environment. They might be hotter or colder than the Earth. They might not have oxygen in their atmospheres. They might not even have water. Could life still exist on worlds like these?

The answer is: perhaps! **Let's explore ...**

The cells of all living things on Earth contain carbon. Carbon atoms can bond with other atoms in many different ways, so they are really good at making the useful chemical reactions that life depends on. **Silicon** makes bonds in a similar way to carbon. Silicon-based life is not possible on Earth because it would react with oxygen in our atmosphere, but it might be possible on another world that lacks oxygen.

Also, liquid methane could be an alternative to liquid water on colder worlds! **Titan** – one of Saturn's moons – has a thick methane atmosphere, so it's possible that Titan might have liquid methane. If there are super-hot vents deep down in Titan's ocean floor, perhaps some life forms might have grown there?

Closer to Earth, the surface of Mars is too cold for liquid water, and the only water we know of on the planet is in the form of ice at the planet's north pole. However, Mars shows signs of old, dried-up riverbeds, and scientists believe that there may have been liquid water on Mars about 4 billion years ago. Does this mean that there might once have been **life on Mars**?

Of course, gravity plays a part too. On higher-gravity worlds such as Jupiter, creatures would likely be shorter and stockier because the higher gravity would make them heavier and they would need to be stronger. An ocean world might give rise to enormous beasts like whales on Earth. A lower-gravity world might have more flying creatures, taking advantage of less pull to the ground.

Now we are planning to send people to live on Mars. Who knows what they might find . . . and who knows how those first emigrants to Mars might evolve . . . from **Earthlings into Martians**!

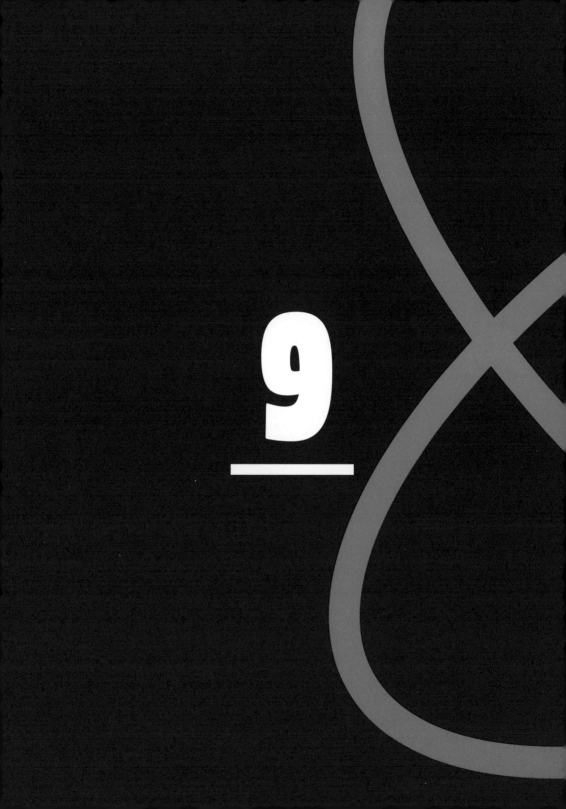

A
UNIVERSE
OF
WONDERS

Dear Diary,

13.8 billion years old

There is so much weird stuff going on inside me! It really would make an awesome tour someday . . . if anyone had a few **billion trillion** years spare to travel

between

all the

different

attractions!

NEXT STOP, THE UNIVERSE?

You may have noticed that in science fiction, humans travel all over the solar system, the galaxy and even the Universe. In real life, this is next to impossible because of the sheer vastness of space.

Take the space probe Voyager 1. It was launched in 1977 and is now travelling through **interstellar space** at 17.3 kilometres per second. Pretty fast, right? But even our nearest star, Proxima Centauri, is 40 billion kilometres away, or 4.25 light years. It would take over **70,000 years** for Voyager 1 to get there! Even if we could travel at the speed of light – which we can't because it would take an impossible amount of energy – the journey would still take us more than four years! But who knows, one day we may figure out how to travel these vast distances much more quickly.

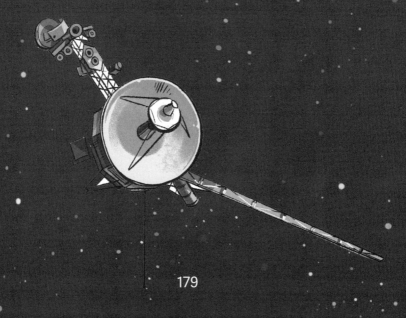

Do stars move?

Proxima Centauri, our nearest neighbouring star, is 'just' 4.25 light years away. But remember, gravity keeps everything moving, and stars spin around the centre of their galaxy just like planets spin around their suns. This means that the distances to different places will change over time. Proxima Centauri and Barnard's Star are both moving in our direction and it's a close race! By the year 11,700 our nearest neighbour star might be Barnard's Star, only 3.8 light years away!

Do you remember how we use light years as an easier way to measure really huge distances? The average distance from the Moon to Pluto is much less than one light year – it's 0.0006 light years, or nearly 5.9 billion kilometres.

So that we don't have to calculate with awkward numbers that are too big or too small, we can also use smaller units of light speed to measure distances inside the solar system: light hours, light minutes or light seconds – the distance a photon of light travels in an hour, a minute or a second . . .

1 light hour = 1.079 billion kilometres
1 light minute = 17.99 million kilometres
1 light second = 299,792 kilometres

THE SEVEN WONDERS OF THE SOLAR SYSTEM

These destinations are close enough to be measured in light minutes and light seconds. Let's dream the impossible — that we can travel at the speed of light. Then you can easily see how quickly we would arrive at these amazing places!

THE GRANDEST CANYON – MARS

3 minutes, 30 seconds away at light speed

The Grand Canyon in Arizona, USA, is magnificently impressive at nearly 450 kilometres long and around 1.6 kilometres deep. But there is a valley on Mars that's more than 4,000 kilometres long, 200 kilometres wide and 7 kilometres deep! Known as Valles Marineris, it runs for almost as long as the entire USA from east to west!

HEXAGONAL STORMS – SATURN

1 hour, 20 minutes away at light speed

The rings of Saturn are truly spectacular and well worth a visit. But while you're visiting this gas giant, take some time to admire the giant hexagonal storm around Saturn's north pole. The sides of this hexagon are 14,500 kilometres long – that's nearly 2,000 kilometres longer than the width of the Earth!

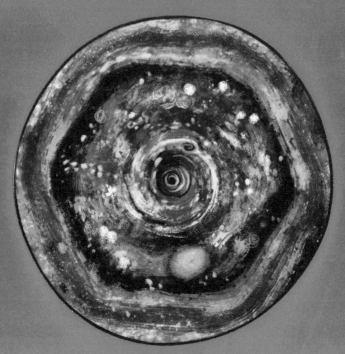

WORST SPOT FOR A HOLIDAY – VENUS

3 minutes, 46 seconds away at light speed

To be fair, there are no 'best' holiday spots in the entire solar system besides Earth. You literally cannot survive anywhere else. But while you can freeze to death, suffocate or burn to a frazzle in a variety of space places, Venus will take just moments to kill you in all sorts of ways. It will roast you (the temperature is around 450 degrees Celsius), squash you (the atmospheric pressure makes it feel like you're about a kilometre deep in the ocean), suffocate you (the air is toxic gas) and dissolve you (it rains sulphuric acid) – all at the same time. Not exactly relaxing, eh?

WEIRDEST DESTINATION – HAUMEA

6 hours away at light speed

Haumea is a dwarf planet that orbits beyond Pluto, and it's a weird old place. Firstly, it's shaped like a squashed rugby ball because it spins so fast. One day on Haumea lasts just four hours! Since it takes 285 Earth years for Haumea to orbit the Sun, there are nearly 625,000 Earth days in Haumea's year – just imagine what a calendar would look like there! Haumea also has a ring around it, has two moons and is covered in water-ice. If you wrapped up warmly enough and carried an oxygen tank, you could ice skate on its surface . . . but that's not a good idea because its gravity is so low that if you fell you would go tumbling a looooong way. If you jumped into the air, you might even reach a height of around seven metres!

Haumea, Pluto and the other dwarf planets beyond Neptune – Eris and Makemake – are known as **plutoids**.

LARGEST CLIFF – MIRANDA

2 hours, 34 minutes away at light speed

The biggest cliff in the solar system (that we know of) can be found on the battered surface of Miranda, which is one of the smaller moons of Uranus. The cliff is called Verona Rupes and reaches a height of 20 kilometres. That's more than twice the height of Mount Everest!

PRETTIEST PLANET – EARTH

0 minutes away at light speed!

Of all the worlds we know of, the Earth is the only one that has life. With its blue oceans, green forests, yellow beaches, white ice caps, and flowers and creatures of every colour, the Earth is like a beautiful and precious jewel hanging in the darkness of space.

BIGGEST VOLCANO – MARS

3 minutes, 30 seconds away at light speed

We've seen Mars' super-deep canyon, but what better place to finish our tour of wonders than with a visit to the biggest volcano in the solar system? Olympus Mons (which means Mount Olympus) is a shield volcano that stands 25 kilometres high – three times higher than Mount Everest – and 624 kilometres wide. That's quite a hike, especially in a spacesuit. Oh, and pick when you visit carefully – this super-volcano could erupt at any moment . . .

I've looked down on the Earth from space, and it's the most amazing sight I've ever seen. It looks so fragile floating in the darkness – I just wish we would look after it better! We can all do things, whether large or small, that will make a difference to the Earth's future. When we recycle or share cars or use public transport, we help preserve the Earth's resources. Big companies can help with this too, by using sustainable energy or helping to look after local communities. We can look after the Earth and look after each other as well.

What are the strangest things in space?

There are many things we believe to be possible in the Universe – we just haven't found them yet. Perhaps one day we will discover moonmoons – that is, moons that orbit a planet's moon. Or micro black holes that are smaller than an atom. Or the first blanet – a planet that orbits a full-size black hole.

But perhaps the most exciting and likely possibility is the discovery that other life forms exist in the Universe . . .

One day we will learn the truth! We have already developed tools like telescopes and used them to understand more of the Universe around us. Now we even put telescopes into different orbits around the Earth so we can see further and in different ways.

In addition to telescopes like **Hubble**, **Chandra** and **Spitzer** (see pages 59–60), which orbit the Earth, we have also placed telescopes much farther out in space – at sweet spots **1.5 million kilometres away** – where objects can orbit the Sun at the same speed as Earth orbits the Sun. The **Herschel** and **Planck** space observatories were sent there, as was the James Webb Space Telescope. They all look at different parts of the electromagnetic spectrum, helping us to **unlock the secrets of the Universe**.

Blanets orbiting a black hole

THE SEVEN (WEIRDEST) WONDERS OF THE UNIVERSE!

Now that we've toured the solar system, it's time to fasten your seatbelts, as we're whizzing even further out to witness seven of the craziest sights in the cosmos ...

THE EYE IN SPACE

700 years away at light speed

In the constellation of Aquarius, the Helix Nebula can be found. As we know, a nebula is a giant cloud of dust and gas in space. The Helix Nebula is cool because it looks like a giant eye, staring out into infinity.

INVISIBLE GIANTS!

More than 20,000 years away at light speed

Astronomers have spotted four planets roughly the size of the Earth whizzing through space near the 'bulge' of gas and stars in the middle of the Milky Way. These planets have no sun of their own to spin around; perhaps they were tugged from their orbit by some cosmic calamity. Now they wander alone through outer space like giant meteors. It is always night on these frozen worlds.

They're also incredibly hard to spot! We see planets in the solar system because of reflected light from our Sun, but rogue planets have a kind of invisibility cloak because they have no sunlight to reflect.

DIAMOND IN THE SKY

50 years away at light speed

In the constellation of Centaurus there is an old and very dim white dwarf star that is mostly made from carbon and oxygen. Some of the carbon atoms in the core of the star have now crystallised into a colossal diamond. It's difficult to know exactly how much of the core has crystallised – possibly a third or perhaps almost all of it – but whatever way you look at it, you're left with a gigantic star diamond, possibly as much as 4,000 kilometres across! When it was discovered in 2004, astronomers named it Lucy after a famous song by The Beatles, 'Lucy in the Sky with Diamonds'.

As white dwarf stars cool down, the light they emit can start to pulse as the changing gravitational and fusion forces keep balancing out. The speed of the light pulses helps us tell how much of the core has crystalised into a diamond. Maybe somewhere in the Universe there's a life form big enough to wear that diamond in a ring!

SUPER SPEEDING STAR
42,000 years away at light speed

LAMOST-HVS1 is a rare hypervelocity star – a huge sun that zooms through space at 1.6 million kilometres per hour (500 kilometres per second!). It burns 4 times hotter and 3,400 times brighter than our own Sun. It is believed that only the huge gravity force of a black hole is strong enough to snag a star that strays too close and sling it away through space at such high speeds.

THE PLANET OF BURNING ICE
30 years away at light speed

Imagine a planet so close to its sun that a year there lasts just over two Earth days . . . A planet with a scorching temperature of over 500 degrees Celsius . . . A planet the size of Neptune but made mostly of ice around a small rocky core . . . Well, that planet exists, and it's called Gliese 436b. But how can ice exist at such incredible temperatures? The reason is that the planet's gravity is so great it stops the ice from melting and floating away as steam. So the ice remains burning hot – hot enough to melt your skin!

THE HOTTEST WORLD
867 years away at light speed

WASP-12b is the hottest known planet in the Milky Way. It is twice the size of Jupiter, the largest planet in our solar system, and a year there lasts just one day! The surface temperature is an incredible 2,200 degrees Celsius, which is hotter than some stars!

THE DEADLY DRUNKEN SPACE CLOUD

25,000 years away at light speed

Sagittarius B2 is a humungous cloud of dust and gas that is so large it would take 150 years for light to travel from one end to the other. There are many different sorts of molecule within the cloud, including three different kinds of alcohol. It also contains the same chemical ingredients that make raspberries smell. But of course NO ONE should be tempted to taste this cloud of alcohol with the raspberry pong – because Sagittarius B2 also contains a type of cyanide that would quickly kill you!

These are just some of the marvellous wonders waiting out there in the Universe. By using our most powerful telescopes and our powerful imaginations, we can 'travel' to all of these amazing places – and so many more – and dream of what they are really like.

But will we ever see these wonders with our own eyes? Perhaps!

After all, the children of today will become the space explorers of the future . . .

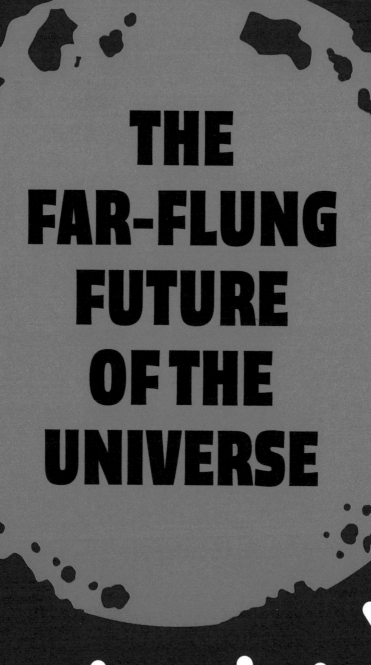

THE
FAR-FLUNG
FUTURE
OF THE
UNIVERSE

Dear Diary,

So, so many years old . . .

Things are getting kind of quiet and chilly around here . . .

I've seen so many exciting and beautiful things. But I also know that all good things must come to an end.

Perhaps even me!

Or, there again, perhaps not . . .

THE SOLAR SYSTEM'S FUTURE

On planet Earth we know that life is precious because it doesn't last for ever. One day, even Earth itself will be gone. But don't worry – we still have billions of years left before that happens! Right now, we're in the twenty-first century. It will be the **fifty-millionth century** before we're in trouble . . .

The problem we face is the very thing that gave us life in the first place – the Sun.

As we know, stars have a lifespan, and our Sun is now middle-aged. Around 5 billion years from now, the Sun will run out of fuel. Its core will collapse and cause its outer layers to expand outwards for millions of miles. Mercury and Venus will be zapped, and the Earth will follow.

But just because Earth will one day go up in smoke, that doesn't mean that humans will go with it!

Are there many universes?

Some astronomers believe that our Universe is just one of many, living side by side – a multiverse. One theory says that there are many universes floating on membranes in a higher dimension, and every now and then they crash into each other, causing Big Bangs.

There are many other theories but none of them have been proved – yet. Maybe YOU will be the one to do it!

IS THERE LIFE IN THE SOLAR SYSTEM?

Groups of humans are already planning to start living on Mars within the next 30 years. Saturn's largest moon, Titan, is another likely spot for humans to set up camp, as it contains many of the essential gases and chemicals needed to support life. Perhaps future humans will harness gravity to shift Earth outward into a new orbit that allows it to survive. There again, as the Sun expands, **Pluto** and the **Kuiper Belt** will grow much warmer so we could always spread out and live on dwarf planets or comets instead!

THE FUTURE OF THE UNIVERSE

For the next several billion years the Universe is likely to stay the same. Only far, far, FAR into the future will things change. It is hard to predict the ultra-distant future of the Universe because there's lots we don't know about it.

- We don't know the shape of it – if it has edges or goes on for ever
- We don't know if it is flat or if it's curved
- We don't know what – if anything – existed before the Big Bang happened

But we *do* know that the fate of the Universe was sealed from the very moment it began. This is because the same laws and forces that made it grow during the Big Bang will also bring about its end.

BIG BANG TO BIG CRUNCH?

Basically, scientists think the Universe will either go on for ever or it will collapse back in on itself.

If the Universe is flat and doesn't contain much matter, then it is an **open universe**. It will go on expanding for ever. But it will also grow colder and emptier as the limited amount of matter is used up over trillions and trillions of years. For instance, a trillion years after the Big Bang, the Milky Way will have used up all its gas and dust and no new stars will be born. In 10 trillion-trillion years the Milky Way will be gone completely. Eventually, so will all other galaxies. Even the **dwarf stars**, **neutron stars** and **black holes** will break down and disappear in the end. The Universe will go on expanding but there will be no more matter left to fill it. There will be nothing but endless empty space.

On the other hand, if the Universe is curved it means that gravity will stop it expanding – it is a **closed universe**. The Universe will start to collapse in on itself; what started with a Big Bang will end with a Big Crunch – like the Big Bang in reverse, with everything squashing down into fiery destruction . . . which might even start off another Big Bang and set a new universe going!

If the future of the Universe sounds a bit bleak, please don't worry — whatever's going to happen will take so much time we can't begin to imagine it. And by then, humans will most likely be smart enough to survive in other forms ANYWHERE!

How will we ever find alien life in the Universe?

We humans are looking and listening hard to find other life in the Universe. We scan the skies for transmissions from alien planets, or search for evidence of alien technology, like lasers firing far away. There is a whole organisation in the USA called SETI – short for Search for Extra-Terrestrial Intelligence. Who knows, maybe YOU will be the first person to discover alien signals in outer space . . .

Dear Diary,

So, so, SO MANY years old . . .

I've grown so big and **sooooooooo ancient**. Those basic laws that govern me – gravity, nuclear forces, electromagnetism – they've been pulling and itching and tickling me for so long I can't tell what the matter is. Or **where** the matter is. Or if the matter really matters (as well as the antimatter, for that matter!).

So, I can't figure out if I'm stretching out for ever and growing chillier all over, or if I've actually started shrinking back in on myself to raise the temperature.

But do you know what? I'm happy either way. So much has happened inside me – so much heat and energy has blasted through my being . . . so many black holes have gulped greedily at my gases . . . so much violent creation and destruction has gone on for so,

SOOOOOO long. If I do exist for ever and ever, it will be good to have a nice rest in the dark and enjoy the peace and quiet. And if I'm going to shrink back in on myself and start another Big Bang, it will be fun to go back and do everything again!

So I'm not putting my diary away just yet. If there's one thing I've learned over the last 999 thousand million billion trillion trillion years, or maybe a little longer, it's that nothing is ever truly gone for good.

Be seeing you, Diary.
Yours, and mine and everyone's,
The Universe xx

AFTERWORD

Here's the thing.
You ARE the Universe.

The particles that make up your body were formed **billions of years ago**, soon after the beginning of time. Those particles have been on quite a journey, travelling through space and time and rearranging themselves many times over until they created **YOU**. You're here, right now. **This is your time**.

And you can think. You can ask questions and search for answers. You are part of the only species we know of that can try to understand the meaning of life. In fact, you could say that it is YOU that gives any meaning to the Universe at all.

And that makes you incredibly special. So **live your life well** and – whatever you do – **use your knowledge wisely**.

Tim Peake

TRAILBLAZING SCIENTISTS FROM AROUND THE WORLD
THE PEOPLE WHO HELPED FURTHER OUR KNOWLEDGE OF SPACE AND EXPLORATION

When we read about the Universe and learn new things, it's thanks to the knowledge of all the discoveries that have come beforehand. We build new knowledge on the old. We replace theories that once seemed to fit with ones that are more likely. In the words of the famous scientist Sir Isaac Newton: 'If I have seen further, it is by standing on the shoulders of giants.' But Newton is just one of so many brilliant people from around the world that have helped us understand the way the Universe works. Here are some others you might like to find out more about. Perhaps one day you will discover new secrets of the Universe by standing on their shoulders.

Gan De (4th century BC)
An ancient Chinese astronomer who conducted observations of Jupiter and created a catalogue of the stars that influenced many later astronomers.

Al-Ma'mun (786–833)
This Persian ruler oversaw the construction of the first observatory in Baghdad. Instead of telescopes it relied on measuring instruments made to a huge scale – some up to 40 metres across!

Abd al-Rahman al-Sufi (903–986)

A pioneering Persian astronomer who organized stars into different types and was the first person known to observe the Andromeda galaxy.

Galileo Galilei (1564–1642)

The Italian scientist, astronomer and engineer who invented the telescope and discovered Jupiter's four biggest moons. His discoveries shaped modern physics and astronomy.

Johannes Kepler (1571–1630)

The German mathematician and astronomer who discovered that the orbits of the planets around the Sun are an ellipse rather than a circle.

Christiaan Huygens (1629–1695)

A Dutch astronomer who discovered Saturn's rings.

Edmond Halley (1656–1742)

This English astronomer analysed the orbits of comets. He was the first person to calculate the orbit of the comet named after him.

Sir Isaac Newton (1642–1727)

The English scientist who was the first to explore the laws of gravity.

William Herschel (1738-1822)

The German-born British astronomer most famous for discovering the planet Uranus – the first planet to be found since ancient times.

Charles Darwin (1809–1882)

An English biologist whose theory of how species change and evolve over time proved to be true and is one of the most influential discoveries of our time.

Ada Lovelace (1815–1852)

The world's first computer programmer – before computers even existed! Born in England, Ada Lovelace predicted the capabilities of modern computers 100 years before they appeared.

Marie Curie (1867–1934)

The Polish-French physicist and mathematician who discovered radioactivity, and who was the first person ever to be awarded two Nobel Prizes.

Henrietta Leavitt (1868–1921)

The American astronomer whose work studying the stars helped scientists to measure the distances to remote galaxies.

Albert Einstein (1879–1955)

The German-born scientist who changed the way we see the Universe with his incredible ideas about gravity and the shape of space-time.

Chandrasekhara Venkata Raman (1888–1970)

This South Indian physicist discovered that when a light beam is scattered by molecules it can change the light's wavelengths. This effect can be used to show us what minerals lie on other planets.

Edwin Hubble (1889–1953)

The American astronomer and astrophysicist whose research helped to prove that the Universe is still expanding.

Meghnad Saha (1893–1956)

The Indian astrophysicist best known for developing the Saha ionization equation, which shows how a star's light spectrum reveals the different elements it contains.

Jan Oort (1900–1992)

This Dutch astronomer proved that the Milky Way galaxy rotates about its centre, but is most famous for predicting the existence of a vast cloud of icy objects orbiting the Sun – now known as the Oort Cloud.

Cecilia Payne-Gaposchkin (1900–1979)

This British-born American astronomer discovered that stars are made mostly of hydrogen and helium.

Gerard Kuiper (1905–1973)

The Dutch-born American astronomer who correctly predicted the existence of a disk-shaped ring of icy objects beyond the orbit of Neptune. This zone was finally discovered in 1992 and named after him.

Subrahmanyan Chandrasekhar (1910–1995)

The Indian-American astrophysicist who discovered that stars larger than 1.4 times the size of our Sun can collapse towards the end of their lives to become neutron stars or black holes, while smaller stars can become white dwarves. This limit of 1.4 times the mass of our Sun is now called the Chandrasekhar Limit.

Chien-Shiung Wu (1912–1997)

The Chinese-American particle and experimental physicist whose 'Wu experiment' proved that identical nuclear particles do not always act in the same way – helping us better understand the weak nuclear force.

Lyman Spitzer Jr. (1914–1997)

The American scientist who was the driving force behind placing an observatory in space, an idea that was realised as the Hubble Space Telescope.

Katherine Johnson (1918–2020)

The now-famous mathematician who worked at NASA as a 'human computer' in the 1960s, calculating orbits and trajectories for spacecraft. Her calculations were key to launching the first Americans into space and the Apollo 11 crew to the Moon and back.

Cyril Andrew Ponnamperuma (1923–1994)

A Sri Lankan chemist who researched the origins of life on Earth, including the role that hot deep sea vents may have played in its development.

Cesare Lattes (1924–2005)

Cesare was a Brazilian experimental physicist whose research included cosmic rays. He helped discover the pion, a subatomic particle that contains a quark and an antiquark.

Meemann Chang (1936–)

The Chinese palaeontologist whose research has increased our understanding of how ancient animals with a backbone evolved from living in the sea to living on land.

Arthur Bertram Cuthbert Walker (1936–2001)
The African American solar physicist who pioneered the development of X-ray and ultraviolet telescopes used to take the first detailed photographs of the Sun's outermost layer.

Roseli Ocampo-Friedmann (1937–2005)
The microbiologist and botanist who studied life in extreme conditions. Filipino-American Roseli's work helped us understand how microorganisms could exist in environments such as that of Mars.

Beatrice Tinsley (1941–1981)
An astronomer and cosmologist from New Zealand whose research has helped our understanding of how galaxies evolve over time.

Stephen Hawking (1942–2018)
An English theoretical physicist who helped us understand gravity, black holes and the beginnings of the Universe.

Jocelyn Bell Burnell (1943–)
An astrophysicist from Northern Ireland who discovered fast-spinning, super-dense neutron stars called **pulsars** that blast radio waves out across the cosmos.

Adriana Ocampo (1955–)
A planetary geologist originally from Colombia, South America, who studies the Earth and other planets, as well as moons, asteroids and comets. She co-discovered the Chicxulub impact crater in Mexico, left by the meteor believed to have wiped out the dinosaurs.

Mae Jemison (1956–)
An astronaut, medical doctor and engineer who became the first African American woman to go into space when she spent more than a week orbiting the Earth as a mission specialist on the space shuttle *Endeavor* in 1992.

Hayashi Saeko (1958–)
Astronomer and founding member of the Japan National Large Telescope project, Hayashi has led cutting-edge astronomical experiments for over 30 years.

Alice Gorman (1964–)
An Australian archaeologist who is internationally recognised for her pioneering work in space archaeology, which is the study of human-made items found in space!

Maggie Ebunoluwa Aderin-Pocock (1968–)
The British space scientist and educator who has designed space instruments including a spectrograph for the Gemini telescope in Chile. She is one of the presenters of the BBC television show, *The Sky at Night.*

Tanya Harrison (1985–)
A US planetary scientist and 'professional Martian', Tanya is an expert on the planet Mars. She has worked on multiple red-planet mission operations for NASA (specialising in Mars rover exploration).

Sabrina Gonzalez Pasterski (1993–)

An American physicist who researches high energy physics. Her work led to the discovery of the 'spin memory effect', which helps to evaluate the effects of gravitational waves.

And there are so many more amazing people to find out about! Who discovered Neptune? Who came up with the name 'Big Bang'? Who was the first person on the Moon? Teachers, search engines, books and libraries can all help you discover more about the Universe – and looking for knowledge makes us all space explorers.

But space agencies around the world don't just need astronauts, astrophysicists and scientists. They need people with a wide range of knowledge and skills – from engineers to maths lovers, writers to artists, doctors to lawyers – and many more. So if you study what you enjoy and work hard, you may well be able to launch your own career into space!

SHOOT FOR THE MOON!

Here are some online sites to help you find out even more exciting information about space and the Universe.

NASA Kids' Club
Interactive games, puzzles, news pages, amazing images and more!

BBC Bitesize KS2 Science
Videos and interactive learning about Earth, space and the solar system from the BBC.

stem.org.uk/esero/tim-peake
Support and resources for teachers on how to use Tim Peake's space mission in the classroom to inspire their pupils to find out more about space.

esa.int/kids/en/learn
Great information for teachers and kids on space and science. Interactive learning and fun things to do.

spotthestation.nasa.gov
Find out when you can spot the International Space Station passing overhead where you live.

GLOSSARY

antimatter: Tiny particles that cannot come into contact with regular matter without going BOOM!

asteroid belt: In our solar system, the region of space between Mars and Jupiter in which most asteroids are found.

asteroids: Small, rocky objects orbiting the Sun.

atmosphere: The layer of gases surrounding a planet or star.

atoms: Tiny particles that make up the basic building blocks of all matter in the Universe.

Big Bang: The idea that the Universe began as a single point, then expanded rapidly.

Big Crunch: The Big Bang in reverse, with everything in the Universe squashing down into fiery destruction.

black hole: A place in space where the gravity is so strong that it pulls all matter into a tiny space.

blanet: A planet that orbits a full-size black hole.

brown dwarf: An object that is smaller than a star and bigger than a planet.

cell: The basic building block of animals and plants.

comet: A ball-shaped mass, orbiting the Sun, that is made up of frozen gases, rocks, dust and ice.

constellation: A group of visible stars that, when viewed from Earth, form a pattern in the sky.

cosmic inflation: The fast expansion of the early Universe after the Big Bang.

Cosmic Microwave Background (CMB): Leftover radiation from the Big Bang.

cosmic rays: High-energy particles that move through space close to the speed of light.

cosmic year: One complete orbit of the Sun around the centre of the Milky Way galaxy (which is equal to 250 million Earth years).

cosmologist: Someone who studies cosmology – the origin and development of the Universe.

cosmos: The entire physical Universe.

dark energy: A form of energy that produces a force which acts in the opposite direction to gravity.

dark matter: Matter made of particles that don't reflect, emit or absorb light.

dwarf planet: A planet-like object, orbiting the Sun, that is smaller than the planet Mercury.

electromagnetic spectrum: The entire range of all types of electromagnetic radiation that exist – gamma rays, X-rays, ultraviolet radiation, visible light, infrared radiation, microwaves and radio waves.

electromagnetism: Interaction between electricity and magnetism.

event horizon: The part of a black hole where light cannot escape.

evolution: The way something develops, adapts and changes over time.

exoplanets: Any planet beyond our solar system orbiting a star that is not our Sun.

galaxy: A collection of stars, gas, dust and dark matter, all held loosely together by gravity.

gravity: The force of attraction that pulls things together.

infinity: The concept of something that is unlimited or endless.

interstellar space: The space between stars in a galaxy.

Kuiper Belt: A ring of ice, icy rocks and comets at the edge of the solar system, beyond the orbit of Neptune.

Laniakea Supercluster: A supercluster of galaxies that includes the Milky Way and approximately 100,000 other nearby galaxies.

light: A type of energy that travels as electromagnetic waves.

light year: The distance light travels in one year.

Local Group: The group of more than 20 galaxies that includes the Milky Way and the Andromeda galaxy.

mass: The amount of matter in an object.

matter: Anything that has mass and takes up physical space.

meteors: Meteoroids that enter Earth's atmosphere and burn brightly due to friction with air. Also called shooting stars.

meteorites: Meteors that don't burn up completely and manage to land on Earth.

meteoroids: Very small asteroids, less than a metre across.

Milky Way: Our galaxy.

moonmoons: Moons that orbit a planet's moon.

nebula: A giant cloud of dust and gas in space.

neutron star: The collapsed core of a giant star.

nuclear force: The force that holds particles together in an atomic nucleus.

nuclear fusion: The fusing together of protons and neutrons to make nuclei.

observable Universe: How much of the Universe we can see through our most powerful telescopes.

Oort Cloud: A region at the furthest reaches of our solar system.

orbit: The continuous movement of one object revolving around another.

particles: Small bits of matter that make up everything in the Universe.

periodic table: A table of all the elements arranged in order of atomic number.

photons: Particles of light energy made of electrical and magnetic waves.

photosynthesis: The process by which plants make food from water and carbon dioxide, using light energy from the Sun.

planetesimals: Small, rocky objects formed when ice, dust and dirt clump together.

plasma: A hot, dense gassy mixture of atomic nuclei and electrons.

plutoid: A dwarf planet that orbits the Sun beyond the orbit of Neptune.

pulsar: A neutron star that spins very fast.

quark: One of a group of tiny particles which, when they combine, form other particles such as hadrons, protons and neutrons.

solar system: A sun and the planets that move around it.

star: A large ball of hot burning matter in space.

supernova: The explosion of a star at the end of its life.

INDEX

PERIODIC TABLE OF THE ELEMENTS

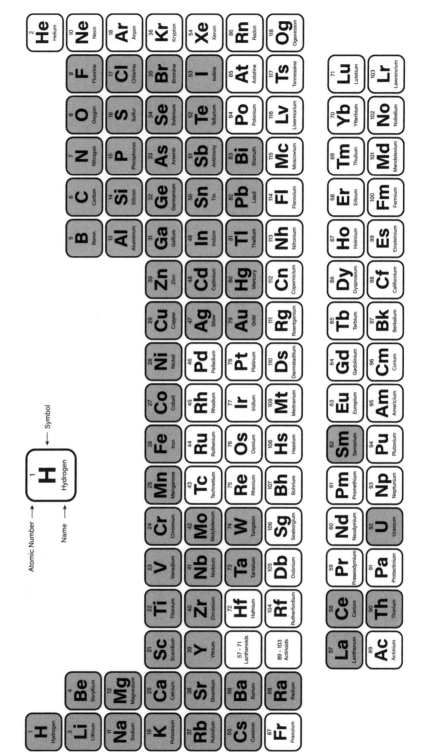

The shaded elements can all be found inside the human body in different amounts – see page 99.